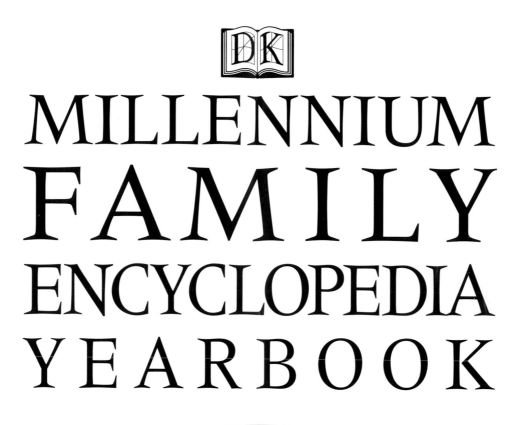

MILLENNIUM FAMILY ENCYCLOPEDIA YEARBOOK

THE MILLENNIUM FAMILY ENCYCLOPEDIA YEARBOOK

DORLING KINDERSLEY

London • New York • Sydney • New Delhi

A DORLING KINDERSLEY BOOK

DK www.dk.com

Senior Editors Maggie Crowley,
Giles Sparrow
Senior Art Editor Cheryl Telfer
Editor Kathleen Bada
Designer Darren Holt

DTP Designer Nomazwe Madonko
Production Kate Oliver

Managing Editor Jayne Parsons
Managing Art Editor Gillian Shaw
Senior DTP Designer Mathew Birch

Picture Research
Louise Edgeworth, Val Mulcahy,
Jo Walton

DK Picture Library
Richard Dabb, Lee Thompson

Jacket Design Andy Smith
Illustrators Sallie Alane Reason,
John Woodcock
Modelmaker Peter Griffiths

For Grant-Laing Partnership
Editors Reg Grant, Jane Laing,
Lee Stacey
Art Editor Ruth Shane

Contributors
Simon Adams, Theresa Greenaway,
Ann Kramer, Cynthia O'Neill,
Louise Pritchard,
Theodore Rowland-Entwistle,
Philip Wilkinson

First published in Great Britain in 1999
by Dorling Kindersley Limited,
9, Henrietta Street,
Covent Garden, London WC2E 8PS

A CIP catalogue for this book is available from the
British Library.

ISBN 0-7513-5789-7

Colour reproduction by Colourscan, Singapore
Printed and bound in China
by L.Rex Printing Company Ltd.

CONTENTS

1997

Dolly the cloned sheep
revolutionizes genetics –
see GENETICS AND
MEDICINE.

Britain goes into
mourning after the
death of Diana – see
DIANA, PRINCESS
OF WALES.

Fireworks
illuminate the
sky as Hong
Kong returns to
China – see
KEY EVENTS
OF 1997.

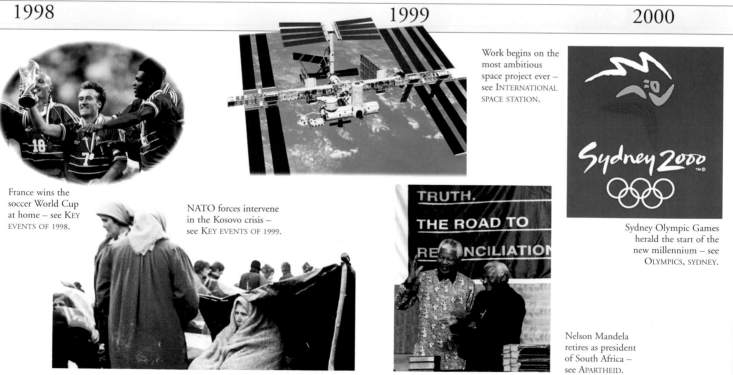

1998

France wins the soccer World Cup at home – see KEY EVENTS OF 1998.

1999

Work begins on the most ambitious space project ever – see INTERNATIONAL SPACE STATION.

NATO forces intervene in the Kosovo crisis – see KEY EVENTS OF 1999.

2000

Sydney 2000

Sydney Olympic Games herald the start of the new millennium – see OLYMPICS, SYDNEY.

Nelson Mandela retires as president of South Africa – see APARTHEID.

HOW TO USE THIS BOOK

THE MILLENNIUM ENCYCLOPEDIA YEARBOOK is divided into three main sections – an update of recent events, an A-Z encyclopedia supplement, and a comprehensive collection of biographies for important figures. To find the entry you want, simply turn to the correct letter of the alphabet, consult the contents list, or check in the index at the back of the yearbook. The A-Z pages follow the same design as entries in the main encyclopedia, and the sticker system allows easy cross-referencing to and from the yearbook. The biographies and updates cover specific subjects in more detail, and again make use of the sticker system.

SOUTH AFRICAN LEADERS

South Africa's political leaders were its prime ministers until 1984, and presidents after that date.

1910–19	Louis Botha
1919–24	Jan Christian Smuts
1924–39	James Hertzog
1939–48	Jan Christian Smuts
1948–54	Daniel Malan
1954–58	Johannes Strijdom
1958–66	Hendrik Verwoerd
1966–78	B. J. Vorster
1978–89	P. W. Botha
1989–94	F. W. De Klerk
1994–99	Nelson Mandela
1999–	Thabo Mbeke

Thabo Mbeke

Reference section
The reference spread at the back of the encyclopedia contains updates to the information in the *DK Millennium Family Encyclopedia's* reference section (Volume 5). It also contains new reference boxes covering additional subjects.

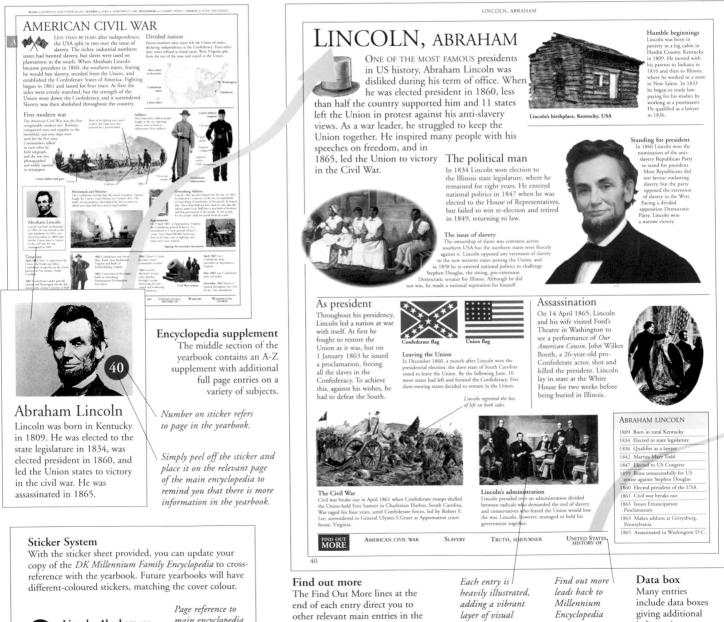

Encyclopedia supplement
The middle section of the yearbook contains an A-Z supplement with additional full page entries on a variety of subjects.

Abraham Lincoln
Lincoln was born in Kentucky in 1809. He was elected to the state legislature in 1834, was elected president in 1860, and led the Union states to victory in the civil war. He was assassinated in 1865.

Number on sticker refers to page in the yearbook.

Simply peel off the sticker and place it on the relevant page of the main encyclopedia to remind you that there is more information in the yearbook.

Sticker System
With the sticker sheet provided, you can update your copy of the *DK Millennium Family Encyclopedia* to cross-reference with the yearbook. Future yearbooks will have different-coloured stickers, matching the cover colour.

40 Lincoln, Abraham *see* American Civil War p. 48

Page reference to main encyclopedia

Find out more
The Find Out More lines at the end of each entry direct you to other relevant main entries in the encyclopedia. Using the Find Out More lines can help you understand an entry in its wider context.

Each entry is heavily illustrated, adding a vibrant layer of visual information.

Find out more leads back to Millennium Encyclopedia entries.

Data box
Many entries include data boxes giving additional information on a subject.

Biography spreads
The last section of the yearbook contains nearly 100 biographies describing the lives and historical significance of some of the most influential figures in politics, the arts, and science.

Data box summarizing the life of explorer Bartolomeu Dias

Recent events spreads
The front section of the yearbook contains update spreads, covering key world events since the original *DK Millennium Family Encyclopedia* was published, as well as spreads on major scientific advances and issues affecting the world today.

Introduction   *Sub-entry*

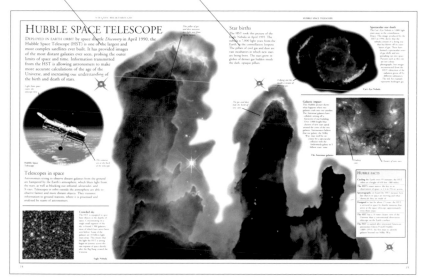

HUBBLE SPACE TELESCOPE

Article structure
Each article begins with a concise introduction and summary. Most information is given in the sub-entries, but some articles are divided into sections covering major areas of interest. Related topics such as biographies are covered in separate boxes.

UNITED STATES, HISTORY OF

Annotation
The illustrations are comprehensively annotated to draw attention to details of particular interest and to explain complex points.

Timeline gives important dates in the history of a subject.

Original encyclopedia
Find Out More lines at the bottom of the Yearbook's encyclopedia supplement entries lead back to relevant subjects in the main *DK Millennium Family Encyclopedia*.

FOREWORD

Welcome to the first *Yearbook* for the *DK Millennium Family Encyclopedia*. This *Yearbook* is an annual publication, designed to keep you up-to-date with everything happening in the world today. Each new yearbook will enrich and enhance the *Millennium Family Encyclopedia*, the only encyclopedia specially created for the visual age of television, video, and multimedia.

Children today live in a highly visual world, much of it compelling and distracting. DK's integration of words and pictures brings the same kind of excitement to information as entertainment does – and learning becomes fun. Over the years the *Millennium* and its yearbooks will grow into an extraordinary reference work for this highly visual information age, enabling your family to continue to build up a comprehensive, up-to-the-moment resource which can be used for both home and project work.

Millennium's Yearbook combines easy reference pages on recent events and scientific breakthroughs with new A-Z entries in the style of the original encyclopedia. It also contains a biography section covering almost 100 influential figures in more detail.

To link the *Yearbook* with the main encyclopedia, we have devised a unique sticker system which will cross-reference any new information to existing articles in the encyclopedia, allowing the books to work together as a powerful information tool. The extensive cross-referencing system teaches children to develop fundamental research skills as they use the index, gazetteer, and *Find Out More* boxes.

I hope that you and your family will continue to benefit from and enjoy the *DK Millennium Family Encyclopedia* for many years to come. The annual *Yearbook* will ensure that this valuable resource remains absolutely up-to-date as well as a highly motivational learning tool for all the family.

Peter Kindersley, Chairman, Dorling Kindersley

KEY EVENTS OF 1997

ALL OTHER EVENTS of 1997 were overshadowed by the tragic death of Diana, Princess of Wales, in a road accident in Paris. Divorced from Prince Charles in 1996, the Princess was with her companion, Dodi Fayed, when their car crashed at high speed in an underpass on the night of 30–31 August. Diana was remembered as the "People's Princess", because of her commitment to charitable causes and her ability to touch the feelings of ordinary people. Although she was only 36 when she died, her glamour and turbulent private life had made her the most famous woman in the world.

Mourning a Princess

The death of Diana, Princess of Wales, was followed by an unprecedented tide of public grief. The areas in front of royal palaces in London were turned into shrines as people covered them with tributes including flowers, poems, and personal momentos. The Princess's funeral, held on 6 September, brought Britain to a halt, and was watched by millions on television around the globe.

Fireworks explode across Hong Kong to celebrate the handover of the colony to China.

Tributes to Diana outside Kensington Palace

China takes over Hong Kong

On 1 July, Britain handed over its colony of Hong Kong to the People's Republic of China. The British had ruled Hong Kong island since 1842, but the New Territories, which made up the bulk of the colony on the mainland, had only been acquired from China on a 99-year lease in 1898, so in 1997 the lease was up. Hong Kong is a major world centre of trade and finance – the Communist government of the People's Republic pledged to allow business to continue as usual for at least 50 years.

New prime minister Tony Blair

The Blair family after the election

Blair is elected

A general election held in Britain on 1 May resulted in a landslide victory for New Labour, led by the dynamic Tony Blair. Aged 43, Blair became Britain's youngest prime minister in 185 years. His victory ended an 18-year period of Conservative government. New Labour won 419 of the 659 seats in the House of Commons, giving them the largest majority of any political party since World War II. The new prime minister told the British people: "You have put your trust in me and I intend to repay that trust. I will not let you down".

THE YEAR AT A GLANCE

19 February Deng Xiaoping, leader of the People's Republic of China for almost 20 years, dies at the age of 92.

24 February Scientists at the Roslin Institute, Edinburgh, announce that they have cloned a sheep using a cell from an adult animal.

27 March The bodies of 39 members of the "Heaven's Gate" cult are found at San Diego, California. They had committed suicide believing that a spacecraft was coming to take them to a "level above human".

15 July A leading Italian fashion designer, Gianni Versace, is shot dead outside his mansion in Miami, Florida.

15 October Driving the *Thrust SSC* jet car, British pilot Andy Green sets a new world land-speed record, averaging 1,227 km/h (763 mph) over two timed runs.

31 December Weather experts say that 1997 was the warmest year ever recorded, thus seeming to confirm the theory that "global warming" is taking place.

Death of a saint

Mother Teresa, the Albanian-born Roman Catholic nun who became a living legend for her tireless devotion to the poor, died aged 87 in her adopted home, Calcutta, India, on 5 September. Mother Teresa founded the religious order of the Missionaries of Charity to help her in her work. She was awarded the Nobel Peace Prize in 1979.

Mother Teresa lies in state.

Exploring the Red Planet

On 4 July, Independence Day in the United States, the American *Pathfinder* space probe landed on the surface of Mars. It was the first landing on the planet since 1976. *Pathfinder* was carrying a remote-controlled buggy, *Sojourner*, which was used to explore the ground around the landing site, collecting and analyzing samples of rocks and soil.

Young Master

Eldrick "Tiger" Woods was only 21 years old in April when he won the most prestigious golf tournament in the world, the US Masters. He was the youngest player ever to win the Masters, and he also recorded the best score in the competition's history, at 18 under par. Woods had been a child prodigy – he appeared on national television to show off his golfing skills at the tender age of 2.

Tiger Woods, Masters' victor

Louise Woodward hears the guilty verdict.

Disputed trial of British teenager

On 30 October, a jury in Boston, Massachusetts, found 19-year-old British girl Louise Woodward guilty of the murder of baby Matthew Eappen. The baby had been left in Woodward's care by his parents, who were employing her as an *au pair*. Woodward hotly denied the charge. The trial judge, Hiller Zobel, later changed the verdict to manslaughter and allowed her immediate release.

KEY EVENTS OF 1998

THE NEWS in 1998 was dominated by scandal in the United States. After an initial public denial, President Bill Clinton was forced to admit that he had had an affair with a young White House intern, Monica Lewinsky. The president's political opponents sought to exploit the scandal to drive him from office, but he remained unshakeably popular with the American people. Elsewhere, the Good Friday agreement brought hope of peace to Northern Ireland, but Central America was devastated by Hurricane Mitch.

David Trimble (left) and John Hume (right) with singer Bono of U2

Good Friday agreement

On 10 April, Good Friday, Protestant and Catholic parties in Northern Ireland reached an agreement to end 30 years of sectarian conflict. Voters approved the agreement in a referendum and Unionist leader David Trimble was later elected head of a power-sharing government in the province. Trimble and Social Democrat John Hume were jointly awarded the Nobel Peace Prize for their part in the peace process.

France triumphs in the World Cup

The 1998 soccer World Cup tournament ended in scenes of mass celebration after the home side, France, defeated the holders, Brazil, in the final. The French owed their 3-0 victory to two goals by Zinedine Zidane and another by Emmanuel Petit. Brazil's striker Ronaldo, regarded as the top footballer in the world, was taken ill just before the match and performed very poorly. In general, the staging of the tournament in France was judged a success, despite some violent clashes between French police and hooligans from England and from Germany.

French players celebrate their victory.

Monica Lewinsky

President Clinton remained popular with Americans.

The Lewinsky affair

In September, prosecutor Kenneth Starr delivered his report on President Clinton's affair with Monica Lewinsky to Congress. The president's videotaped testimony was broadcast nationwide, and Starr called for the president to be impeached for lying under oath. In December, contrary to the wishes of most Americans, Congress impeached the president, although he was later acquitted.

Veteran returns to space

On 29 October, John Glenn, a US senator for Ohio, became the oldest person ever launched into space. The 77-year-old veteran astronaut took off from Cape Canaveral as one of the seven-strong crew of the space shuttle *Discovery*. Over 250,000 people turned out to witness the launch. The nine-day shuttle mission was Glenn's second space voyage, and was used to study the effects of age in space. Glenn had already entered the history books in 1962 as the first American to orbit the Earth, aboard the space capsule *Friendship 7*. On that occasion his flight lasted a mere five hours.

Astronaut John Glenn

Sphinx restored

In May, archaeologists completed a 10-year project to restore one of the most famous monuments of ancient Egypt, the Sphinx at Giza. The restoration was celebrated by a laser lightshow that illuminated the Sphinx in spectacular colours. Traffic pollution from nearby Cairo is blamed for the recent deterioration of the Sphinx, which has survived for 5,000 years.

The sphinx lit by lasers

Titanic equals Oscar record

As well as being a massive box-office hit, the disaster movie *Titanic* triumphed at the Oscars in March. It took a total of 11 Academy Awards, equalling the record set in 1960 by the epic *Ben Hur*. The awards included best picture, and best director for James Cameron. The Oscar winners did not, however, include the movie's youthful heart-throb stars Leonardo DiCaprio and Kate Winslet. DiCaprio, currently the hottest property in Hollywood, pointedly stayed away from the Academy Awards ceremony after his failure to win a nomination.

Leonardo DiCaprio

Kate Winslet

Hurricane Mitch

In October and November, vast areas of Honduras and Nicaragua, countries in Central America, were devastated by Hurricane Mitch. It was the fourth strongest hurricane to strike the Caribbean region in the 20th century. The worst damage was caused by torrential rain, with up to 60 cm (24 in) falling daily over a five-day period. Towns and villages were buried by landslides, while flooding swept away roads and bridges. At least 10,000 people are believed to have died in the catastrophe, and more than a million were left homeless. Foreign countries rushed to offer aid to the region, but economic recovery will take many years.

Refugees made homeless by Hurricane Mitch

THE YEAR AT A GLANCE

14 May American singer and actor Frank Sinatra dies at the age of 82.

20 May Prolonged popular protests force President Suharto of Indonesia to resign.

28 May Pakistan explodes a series of nuclear devices in response to similar nuclear weapons tests by India.

7 August Terrorist bomb attacks by Islamic extremists on US embassies in Kenya and Tanzania kill more than 250 people.

15 August A car-bomb explosion in a busy shopping street in Omagh, Northern Ireland, kills 28 people and injures hundreds more.

9 September Mark McGwire of the St. Louis Cardinals breaks the record for the most home runs in a baseball season with his 62nd homer. The record had stood since 1961.

24 September Novelist Salmon Rushdie is told that the Iranian government is lifting the *fatwah* (Islamic decree) offering a reward for his assassination as a blasphemer.

KEY EVENTS OF 1999

THE LAST YEAR of the millennium was marred by the war that broke out between the NATO powers and Serbia. At issue was the future of the Serb-ruled province of Kosovo, where ethnic Albanian guerrillas were fighting Serbian forces. When Serbian leader Slobodan Milosevic refused to accept a peace agreement on Kosovo in March, NATO began air attacks that soon escalated into large-scale military involvement.

Kosovo suffers "ethnic cleansing"

When NATO aircraft started their raids on Yugoslavia in March, the Serbian forces inside Kosovo embarked on a systematic campaign of "ethnic cleansing", driving Albanians from their homes and forcing them to flee the country. Many were massacred, while hundreds of thousands fled to neighbouring countries. The NATO allies struggled to provide the refugees with food and temporary shelter.

Kosovan refugees in a makeshift camp

The Queen visiting Australia in 1992

Australia to be a republic?

In November, a referendum will determine whether Australia is to keep the Queen of England as head of state or to become a republic with an appointed president. If voters approve proposals that were drawn up by a Constitutional Convention in February 1998, the country will be declared a republic on 1 January 2001. The Queen has already suffered one rebuff – she has not been asked to open the Sydney Olympic Games in the year 2000.

Europe embraces the euro

On 1 January, 11 European Union countries with a combined population of 290 million launched a single currency, known as the "euro". Euro notes and coins were set to replace national currencies in everyday use in the year 2002. The only EU countries staying outside the "euro zone" were Britain, Denmark, Sweden, and Greece. Closer political union between the euro-zone states seems certain to follow hard on the heels of monetary union.

Euro note and coins

GM protester

Protesters challenge GM foods

In February, protesters in Europe focused attention on the increasingly widespread use of genetically modified (GM) crops in food products. GM crops are a potentially valuable result of progress in genetics, but protesters claim that their possible harmful effects on the environment and on human health have not been adequately tested.

Millennium fever

The beginning of a new millennium on 1 January 2000 will be a moment to make people think of their place in history. Already there is a rush to create "time capsules" for burial, to give future generations an idea of life today. The largest single project for the occasion is the Millennium Dome, built at Greenwich in east London. When complete, the Dome will be by far the largest structure of its kind anywhere in the world – 50 m (165 ft) tall and 1 km (1,100 yd) in circumference. The total cost to build the dome will be £750 million ($1.25 billion).

Greenwich Millennium Dome

Millennium babies

The media has excited interest in the idea of "millennium babies" – babies that will be born on 1 January 2000. Some newspapers actively encouraged would-be parents to attempt to conceive on 17 March, the day most likely to lead to millennium birth.

Night of celebration

People across the globe are planning all-night parties and special events to mark the end of the 20th century and the beginning of a new millennium. Many venues for millennium parties have already been booked. Costs for travel and festivities are expected to rise to unheard-of levels as demand outstrips supply. Some people are hoping to be the first to see the sun rise on the new millennium by travelling as near as possible to the International Date Line that runs down the middle of the Pacific Ocean. The new millennium will begin there 17 hours earlier than in New York and 12 hours earlier than at Greenwich in London.

The Eiffel Tower in Paris is to be one focus of celebrations.

Bugged by the millennium

There are many scenarios for a disaster at the start of the new millennium, most of them centring around problems with computers. Most machines are based on designs going back to the 1980s, and were not designed to recognize the year 2000. If not remedied, this "millennium bug" could have serious consequences, jamming traffic lights, causing breakdowns in air traffic control, or cutting communications lines and power supplies.

HUBBLE SPACE TELESCOPE

This pillar of gas and dust measures one light year from top to bottom.

DEPLOYED IN EARTH ORBIT by space shuttle *Discovery* in April 1990, the Hubble Space Telescope (HST) is one of the largest and most complex satellites ever built. It has provided images of the most distant galaxies ever seen, probing the outer limits of space and time. Information transmitted from the HST is allowing astronomers to make more accurate calculations of the age of the Universe, and increasing our understanding of the lives of stars.

Light from space enters the telescope here.

Hubble Space Telescope

The cameras are at the back of the telescope.

Telescopes in space

Astronomers trying to observe distant galaxies from the ground are hampered by the Earth's atmosphere, which blurs light from the stars, as well as blocking out infrared, ultraviolet, and X-rays. Telescopes in orbit outside the atmosphere are able to observe fainter and more distant objects. They transmit information to ground stations, where it is processed and analyzed by teams of astronomers.

Crowded sky

The HST is equipped to spot faint objects in the depths of space. Concentrating on a single small segment of the sky, it found 1,500 galaxies, most of which have never been seen before. Some of the galaxies are 10 billion light years away. This means that the light the HST is seeing began its journey across the vast expanse of space shortly after the Big Bang created the Universe.

Eagle Nebula

Star births

The HST took this picture of the
Eagle Nebula in April 1995. The
nebula is 7,000 light years from the
Earth, in the constellation Serpens.
The pillars of cool gas and dust are
vast incubators in which new stars
are being born. The stars grow in
globes of denser gas hidden inside
the dark, opaque pillars.

Spectacular star death

The Cat's Eye Nebula is 3,000 light
years away in the constellation
Draco. This image, produced by the
HST in 1994, shows that the
nebula consists of a dying star
that has blown off its outer
layers of gas. These have
formed a spectacular series
of gas shells and jets
spreading out into space.
Pictures such as this one
are not colour
photographs, but images
reconstructed from the
HST's detection of the
radiation given off by
different substances.
The red, for example,
represents hydrogen gas.

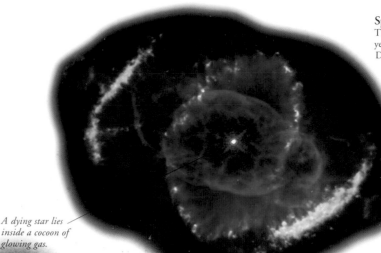

*A dying star lies
inside a cocoon of
glowing gas.*

Cat's Eye Nebula

*The gas and dust
hide the birth of
new stars.*

Galactic impact

This Hubble picture shows
what happens when two
galaxies crash into one another.
The Antennae galaxies have
collided, setting off a firestorm
of star building. Over 1,000
bright blue clusters of new
stars spiral around the cores
of the two galaxies.
Astronomers believe that our
galaxy, the Milky Way, may
itself be on course for a
spectacular collision with
the Andromeda galaxy
in 5 billion years' time.

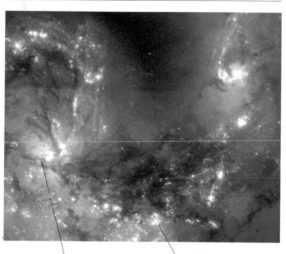

The Antennae galaxies

*Galaxy
core*

Clusters of new stars

HUBBLE FACTS

Circling the Earth every 95 minutes, the HST
orbits at a height of 610 km (380 miles).

The HST's main mirror, the key to its
observation of space, is 2.4 m (94 in) across.

Spectrographs on board the HST measure how
fast objects in space are moving and what
chemicals they are made of.

Designed to last for about 15 years, the HST
is serviced in space by shuttle missions that
arrive at the space telescope approximately
every three years.

The HST has a 10 times clearer view of the
Universe than a conventional observatory
telescope on the Earth's surface.

The HST is named after renowned American
astronomer Edwin Powell Hubble
(1889–1953), the first man to identify
galaxies beyond our Milky Way.

GENETICS AND MEDICINE

THE MOST SENSATIONAL area of scientific progress at the end of the millennium has been in genetics. As scientists have begun to understand the details of genetic material, they have begun to understand how to change it in order to alter life itself. Cloning – the reproduction of identical animals grown from single cells – is immensely controversial, because it opens up the possibility of humans making exact copies of themselves. Human cloning has already been banned in many countries.

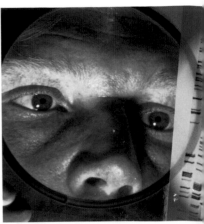

A print-out of gene sequences

Dolly the cloned sheep

Send in the clones

The first cloning experiments involved the duplication of animals from embryo cells – effectively creating artificial twins. In 1996, scientists at Scotland's Roslin Institute created a clone using a cell from an adult sheep. The resulting animal, Dolly, was presented to the world in 1997. Dolly instantly became a global celebrity, sparking off a fierce debate about the ethics of clones. More recently, scientists have discovered that Dolly's cells may be aging faster than normal, raising questions about how practical cloning of human beings would be.

A single cell divides to begin the creation of a clone.

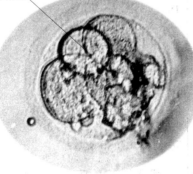

Identical mice cloned from the first mouse's genes

Original mouse from which genetic material was taken for cloning

Mice cloned at the University of Hawaii

Cloned mice
In 1998, researchers at the University of Hawaii announced that they had cloned three generations of mice – more than 50 identical animals, including clones of clones. Cloning is currently being used to reproduce genetically modified animals that will provide organs for transplanting into humans and drugs for medical use.

Human Genome Project

Since 1990, a large number of researchers worldwide have been engaged on the Human Genome Project, an attempt to map every one of the roughly 80,000 genes that together make up the blueprint for an individual human being. The researchers intend to identify what each gene does and how it relates to all the other genes. Progress in human genetics is already making it theoretically possible to modify human embryos in order to eliminate specific hereditary diseases. Ultimately, it may be possible to change any aspect of an individual before birth – in effect, to make a baby with any characteristic that its parents may choose, from blue eyes to high intelligence.

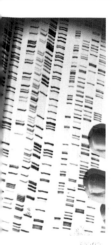

Bionic arm

A bionic arm is an artificial limb that can be controlled directly by thoughts in the brain. A team at the Princess Margaret Rose Hospital in Edinburgh, Scotland, has developed a bionic arm that is crammed with microchips. At the point where the arm is attached to the patient's shoulder, its sensors pick up electrical pulses from the brain. The arm's electronics interpret these pulses and convert them into the normal range of arm movements through battery-powered gears and pulleys. The inner workings of the arm are usually hidden by a wipe-clean skin-coloured silicone surface.

Genetically modified foods

Genetic modification (GM) involves taking a gene from one plant or animal and inserting it into the genetic material of another organism. Scientists have been using this technique to produce crops that grow better and are more profitable – for example, they may be resistant to pests. A wide range of GM crops, including maize, tomatoes, and potatoes, are now being grown. Critics argue that the effects of GM are dangerously unpredictable. They claim that GM crops could damage the environment and that GM foods may harm human immune systems. Most scientists dismiss these claims, saying that GM foods will help to feed the world's growing population.

Sensors on fingers return feedback to the wearer.

Hand sewn on

In September 1998, Clint Hallam, a New Zealand businessman living in Australia, became the first person to have a hand transplant. Hallam had lost his hand in an accident with a circular saw in 1984. An international team of surgeons at the Edouard Herriot hospital in Lyons, France, removed a hand from another patient who had been declared brain-dead and sewed it onto the stump of Hallam's arm. It took 13 hours to connect all the nerves, muscles, tendons, and arteries of the arm to the hand.

The hand grips gently but firmly.

Clint Hallam's new hand

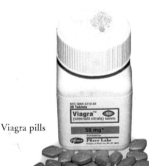

Viagra pills

Motors controlled by electrical signals from the brain.

Viagra breakthrough

The most newsworthy medical breakthrough of the late 1990s was the development of Viagra, a pill designed to cure sexual impotence, a condition that may affect one man in ten. Viagra was a by-product of research into the role of nitric oxide in the body. American scientists Robert Furchgott, Louis Ignarro, and Ferid Murad found that nitric oxide acts as a "messenger" allowing cells inside the body to communicate with one another. They also discovered that nitric oxide plays a crucial role in male sexual functioning. The three scientists were awarded the Nobel Prize for medicine. In 1998, American doctors wrote 25,000 prescriptions for Viagra every day.

PROGRESS IN GENETICS

1953 Scientists James Watson and Francis Crick discover the structure of DNA (deoxyribonucleic acid), the material from which genes are made.

1981 Insulin is produced by bacteria, the first commercial product of genetic engineering.

1983 The first genetically modified (GM) crops are created.

1984 The technique known as "genetic fingerprinting" is developed. This allows scientists to identify an individual from a sample of his or her DNA.

1990 The Human Genome Project begins, with the aim of identifying and analyzing all the genes in a human cell.

1997 Scientists announce that a sheep called Dolly is the first animal cloned from a cell taken from an adult animal.

2003 Projected date for the completion of the Human Genome Project.

INTERNATIONAL SPACE STATION

IN 1998, work began on the International Space Station (ISS), the biggest space project since the crewed flights to the Moon. The station will take six years to complete, requiring almost 100 rocket launches and over 160 spacewalks. As well as providing space laboratories for scientists to carry out gravity-free experiments and precise observations of the Earth and outer space, the ISS is considered a necessary stepping stone to the next leap in space exploration, a crewed mission to Mars.

The *Zarya* control module

How the ISS will look

When it is completed, the ISS will weigh 460 tonnes and measure 100 m (330 ft) in length. Orbiting at a height of 350 to 500 km (220 to 310 miles), the sunlight reflected off it at night will make it visible to the naked eye from Earth. The ISS will be assembled from about 100 separate units, and will be occupied by three astronauts from midway through its construction. When complete, it will house a rotating crew of seven people.

Sunrise in space

The first section of the ISS put into orbit was the *Zarya* module – Zarya means "sunrise" in Russian. *Zarya* lifted off from Baikonour in Kazakhstan on 20 November 1998, propelled into space by a Russian Proton rocket. The most important features of the module are its solar-panelled wings, which provided the power to bring the station to life once the second module, *Unity*, was linked to it the following month.

Space station Mir

Ageing station

The ISS is the successor to the Soviet space station *Mir*, which has been in crewed orbit around the Earth since 1986. *Mir* has provided much valuable experience in dealing with the problems confronted by astronauts spending long periods of time in weightless conditions. By the late 1990s, however, *Mir* was drawing to the end of its operational life, becoming a dangerously accident-prone vehicle.

Science power platform

Zarya control module

American spacewalkers
Beginning on 7 December 1998, US astronauts Jerry Ross and James Newman carried out a series of spacewalks to link the *Unity* module to the *Zarya* module. *Unity*, taken up to the ISS site by the space shuttle *Endeavour*, has a series of hatches and docking ports that will make it the hub for the assembly of the remainder of the space station.

Unity node module

Photovoltaic arrays (solar cells)

Laboratories and living quarters

Shuttle crew
On 3 December 1998, the space shuttle *Endeavour* set off on the second stage of the ISS project, attaching the *Unity* and *Zarya* modules. This photograph of *Endeavour's* crew shows (left to right) Americans Jerry Ross, Rick Sturckow, James Newman, Nancy Currie, and Robert Cabana, and Russian Sergei Krikalev. Behind them are the flags of the 16 countries involved in the space station project – the United States, Russia, Japan, Brazil, Canada, and the 11 members of the European Space Agency.

The crew of space shuttle *Endeavour*, December 1998

ASSEMBLING THE ISS

November 1998 A Russian Proton rocket sends the *Zarya* control module into orbit.

December 1998 The space shuttle *Endeavour* carries the *Unity* node module into space to link up with the *Zarya* module.

May 1999 An American space shuttle mission attaches a Spacehab double cargo module to the space station.

July 1999 A Russian space vehicle delivers a Service Module to the ISS, containing essential life-support systems.

January 2000 A crew of three American and Russian astronauts are delivered to the ISS. From this time forward, the space station will be permanently crewed.

2004 Projected date for the completion of the assembly of all units of the ISS.

COUNTRIES OF THE WORLD

Afghanistan
Location Asia
Official name Islamic State of Afghanistan
Capital Kabul
Currency Afghani
Main languages Persian and Pashtu
Population 23.4 million

Albania
Location Europe
Official name Republic of Albania
Capital Tirana
Currency Lek
Main language Albanian
Population 3.4 million

Algeria
Location North Africa
Official name Democratic and Popular Republic of Algeria
Capital Algiers
Currency Algerian dinar
Main language Arabic
Population 30.2 million

Andorra
Location Europe
Official name Principality of Andorra
Capital Andorra la Vella
Currency French franc and Spanish peseta
Main language Catalan
Population 65,000

Angola
Location Southern Africa
Official name Republic of Angola
Capital Luanda
Currency Readjusted kwanza
Main language Portuguese
Population 12 million

Antarctica (International territory)
Location South Pole
Official name Antarctica
Capital None
Currency None
Main language None
Population 4,000

Antigua and Barbuda
Location Caribbean
Official name Antigua and Barbuda
Capital St. John's
Currency Eastern Caribbean dollar
Main language English
Population 66,000

Argentina
Location South America
Official name Argentine Republic
Capital Buenos Aires
Currency Argentine peso
Main language Spanish
Population 36.1 million

Armenia
Location Asia
Official name Republic of Armenia
Capital Yerevan
Currency Dram
Main language Armenian
Population 3.6 million

Australia
Location Australasia
Official name Commonwealth of Australia
Capital Canberra
Currency Australian dollar
Main language English
Population 18.4 million

Austria
Location Europe
Official name Republic of Austria
Capital Vienna
Currency Euro and Schilling
Main language German
Population 8.2 million

Azerbaijan
Location Asia
Official name Republic of Azerbaijan
Capital Baku
Currency Manat
Main language Azerbaijani
Population 7.7 million

Bahamas
Location Caribbean
Official name Commonwealth of the Bahamas
Capital Nassau
Currency Bahamian dollar
Main language English
Population 293,000

Bahrain
Location Middle East
Official name State of Bahrain
Capital Manama
Currency Bahrain dinar
Main language Arabic
Population 594,000

Bangladesh
Location South Asia
Official name People's Republic of Bangladesh
Capital Dhaka
Currency Taka
Main language Bengali
Population 124 million

Barbados
Location Caribbean
Official name Barbados
Capital Bridgetown
Currency Barbados dollar
Main language English
Population 263,000

Belgium
Location Europe
Official name Kingdom of Belgium
Capital Brussels
Currency Euro and Belgian franc
Main languages Flemish, French, and German
Population 10.2 million

Belize
Location Central America
Official name Belize
Capital Belmopan
Currency Belizean dollar
Main language English
Population 200,000

Belorussia
Location Eastern Europe
Official name Republic of Belorussia
Capital Minsk
Currency Belarusian rouble
Main language Belarusian
Population 10.3 million

Benin
Location West Africa
Official name Republic of Benin
Capital Porto-Novo
Currency CFA franc
Main language French
Population 5.9 million

Bhutan
Location South Asia
Official name Kingdom of Bhutan
Capital Thimphu
Currency Ngultrum
Main language Dzongkha
Population 1.9 million

Bolivia
Location South America
Official name Republic of Bolivia
Capital Sucre (official); La Paz (administrative)
Currency Boliviano
Main languages Spanish, Aymará, and Quechua
Population 7.4 million

Bosnia and Herzegovina
Location Europe
Official name Republic of Bosnia and Herzegovina
Capital Sarajevo
Currency Bosnian dinar
Main language Serbo-Croat
Population 4 million

Botswana
Location Southern Africa
Official name Republic of Botswana
Capital Gaborone
Currency Pula
Main language English
Population 1.6 million

Brazil
Location South America
Official name Federative Republic of Brazil
Capital Brasília
Currency Real
Main language Portuguese
Population 165.2 million

Brunei
Location Southeast Asia
Official name Sultanate of Brunei
Capital Bandar Seri Begawan
Currency Brunei dollar
Main language Malay
Population 313,000

Bulgaria
Location Europe
Official name Republic of Bulgaria
Capital Sofia
Currency Lev
Main language Bulgarian
Population 8.4 million

Burkina
Location West Africa
Official name Burkina Faso
Capital Ouagadougou
Currency CFA franc
Main language French
Population 11.4 million

La Paz, the administrative capital of Bolivia, South America

Burma (Myanmar)
Location Southeast Asia
Official name Union of Myanmar
Capital Yangon (Rangoon)
Currency Kyat
Main language Burmese
Population 47.6 million

Burundi
Location Central Africa
Official name Republic of Burundi
Capital Bujumbura
Currency Burundi franc
Main languages French and Kirundi
Population 6.6 million

Cambodia

Location Southeast Asia
Official name Kingdom of Cambodia
Capital Phnom Penh
Currency Riel
Main language Khmer
Population 10.8 million

Cameroon

Location West Africa
Official name Republic of Cameroon
Capital Yaoundé
Currency CFA franc
Main languages English and French
Population 14.3 million

Canada

Location North America
Official name Canada
Capital Ottawa
Currency Canadian dollar
Main languages English and French
Population 30.2 million

Cape Verde

Location West Africa
Official name Republic of Cape Verde
Capital Praia
Currency Cape Verde escudo
Main language Portuguese
Population 417,000

Central African Republic

Location Central Africa
Official name Central African Republic
Capital Bangui
Currency CFA franc
Main language French
Population 3.5 million

Chad

Location Central Africa
Official name Republic of Chad
Capital N'Djamena
Currency CFA franc
Main languages Arabic and French
Population 6.9 million

Chile

Location South America
Official name Republic of Chile
Capital Santiago
Currency Chilean peso
Main language Spanish
Population 14.8 million

China

Location East Asia
Official name People's Republic of China
Capital Beijing
Currency Renminbi, usually called the yuan
Main language Mandarin
Population 1.3 billion

Colombia

Location South America
Official name Republic of Colombia
Capital Bogotá
Currency Colombian peso
Main language Spanish
Population 37.7 million

Comoros

Location Indian Ocean
Official name Federal Islamic Republic of the Comoros
Capital Moroni
Currency Comoros franc
Main languages Arabic and French
Population 672,000

Congo

Location West Africa
Official name Republic of the Congo
Capital Brazzaville
Currency CFA franc
Main language French
Population 2.8 million

Congo (Zaïre)

Location Central Africa
Official name Democratic Republic of the Congo
Capital Kinshasa
Currency Congolese franc
Main language French
Population 49.2 million

Costa Rica

Location Central America
Official name Republic of Costa Rica
Capital San José
Currency Costa Rican colón
Main language Spanish
Population 3.7 million

Croatia

Location Europe
Official name Republic of Croatia
Capital Zagreb
Currency Kuna
Main language Croatian
Population 4.5 million

Cuba

Location Caribbean
Official name Republic of Cuba
Capital Havana
Currency Cuban peso
Main language Spanish
Population 11.1 million

Cyprus

Location Europe
Official name Republic of Cyprus
Capital Nicosia
Currency Cyprus pound (Turkish lira in TRNC)
Main languages Greek and Turkish
Population 766,000

Czech Republic

Location Europe
Official name Czech Republic
Capital Prague
Currency Czech koruna
Main language Czech
Population 10.2 million

Denmark

Location Europe
Official name Kingdom of Denmark
Capital Copenhagen
Currency Danish krone
Main language Danish
Population 5.3 million

Djibouti

Location East Africa
Official name Republic of Djibouti
Capital Djibouti
Currency Djibouti franc
Main language Arabic and French
Population 652,000

Dominica

Location Caribbean
Official name Commonwealth of Dominica
Capital Roseau
Currency Eastern Caribbean dollar
Main language English
Population 74,000

Dominican Republic

Location Caribbean
Official name Dominican Republic
Capital Santo Domingo
Currency Dominican Republic peso
Main language Spanish
Population 8.2 million

Ecuador

Location South America
Official name Republic of Ecuador
Capital Quito
Currency Sucre
Main language Spanish
Population 12.2 million

Egypt

Location North Africa
Official name Arab Republic of Egypt
Capital Cairo
Currency Egyptian pound
Main language Arabic
Population 65.7 million

El Salvador

Location Central America
Official name Republic of El Salvador
Capital San Salvador
Currency Salvadorean colón
Main language Spanish
Population 6.1 million

Equatorial Guinea

Location West Africa
Official name Republic of Equatorial Guinea
Capital Malabo
Currency CFA franc
Main language Spanish
Population 430,000

Estonia

Location Europe
Official name Republic of Estonia
Capital Tallinn
Currency Kroon
Main language Estonian
Population 1.4 million

Eritrea

Location East Africa
Official name State of Eritrea
Capital Asmara
Currency Nakfa
Main language Tigrinya
Population 3.5 million

Ethiopia

Location East Africa
Official name Federal Democratic Republic of Ethiopia
Capital Addis Ababa
Currency Ethiopian birr
Main language Amharic
Population 62.1 million

Fiji

Location South Pacific
Official name Republic of Fiji
Capital Suva
Currency Fiji dollar
Main language English
Population 822,000

Finland

Location Europe
Official name Republic of Finland
Capital Helsinki
Currency Euro and Markka
Main languages Finnish and Swedish
Population 5.2 million

France

Location Europe
Official name French Republic
Capital Paris
Currency Euro and French franc
Main language French
Population 58.7 million

Gabon

Location West Africa
Official name Gabonese Republic
Capital Libreville
Currency CFA franc
Main language French
Population 1.2 million

In the Cambodian capital, Phnom Penh, two-wheeled transport flourishes.

Gambia
Location West Africa
Official name Republic of The Gambia
Capital Banjul
Currency Dalasi
Main language English
Population 1.9 million

Georgia
Location Asia
Official name Republic of Georgia
Capital Tbilisi
Currency Lari
Main language Georgian
Population 5.4 million

Germany
Location Europe
Official name Federal Republic of Germany
Capital Berlin
Currency Euro and Deutsche Mark
Main language German
Population 82.4 million

Ghana
Location West Africa
Official name Republic of Ghana
Capital Accra
Currency Cedi
Main language English
Population 18.9 million

Greece
Location Europe
Official name Hellenic Republic
Capital Athens
Currency Drachma
Main language Greek
Population 10.6 million

Grenada
Location Caribbean
Official name Grenada
Capital St. George's
Currency Eastern Caribbean dollar
Main language English
Population 98,600

The castle area of Budapest, Hungary

Guatemala
Location Central America
Official name Republic of Guatemala
Capital Guatemala City
Currency Quetzal
Main language Spanish
Population 11.6 million

Guinea
Location West Africa
Official name Republic of Guinea
Capital Conakry
Currency Franc guinéen (Guinea franc)
Main language French
Population 7.7 million

Guinea-Bissau
Location West Africa
Official name Republic of Guinea-Bissau
Capital Bissau
Currency Guinea peso
Main language Portuguese
Population 1.1 million

Guyana
Location South America
Official name Cooperative Republic of Guyana
Capital Georgetown
Currency Guyana dollar
Main language English
Population 856,000

Haiti
Location Caribbean
Official name Republic of Haiti
Capital Port-au-Prince
Currency Gourde
Main languages French and French creole
Population 7.5 million

Honduras
Location Central America
Official name Republic of Honduras
Capital Tegucigalpa
Currency Lempira
Main language Spanish
Population 6.1 million

Hungary
Location Europe
Official name Republic of Hungary
Capital Budapest
Currency Forint
Main language Hungarian
Population 9.9 million

Iceland
Location Europe
Official name Republic of Iceland
Capital Reykjavík
Currency Icelandic króna
Main language Icelandic
Population 277,000

India
Location South Asia
Official name Republic of India
Capital New Delhi
Currency Indian rupee
Main languages Hindi and English
Population 976 million

Indonesia
Location Southeast Asia
Official name Republic of Indonesia
Capital Jakarta
Currency Rupiah
Main language Bahasa Indonesia
Population 206.5 million

Iran
Location Middle East
Official name Islamic Republic of Iran
Capital Tehran
Currency Iranian rial
Main language Farsi (Persian)
Population 73.1 million

Iraq
Location Middle East
Official name Republic of Iraq
Capital Baghdad
Currency Iraqi dinar
Main language Arabic
Population 21.8 million

Ireland
Location Europe
Official name Republic of Ireland
Capital Dublin
Currency Euro and Punt
Main languages Irish and English
Population 3.6 million

Israel
Location Middle East
Official name State of Israel
Capital Jerusalem
Currency New Israeli shekel
Main languages Hebrew and Arabic
Population 5.9 million

Italy
Location Europe
Official name Italian Republic
Capital Rome
Currency Euro and Italian lira
Main language Italian
Population 57.2 million

Ivory Coast
Location West Africa
Official name Republic of Côte d'Ivoire
Capital Yamoussoukro
Currency CFA franc
Main language French
Population 14.6 million

Jamaica
Location Caribbean
Official name Jamaica
Capital Kingston
Currency Jamaican dollar
Main language English
Population 2.5 million

Japan
Location East Asia
Official name Japan
Capital Tokyo
Currency Yen
Main language Japanese
Population 125.9 million

Jordan
Location Middle East
Official name Hashemite Kingdom of Jordan
Capital Amman
Currency Jordanian dinar
Main language Arabic
Population 6 million

Kazakhstan
Location Asia
Official name Republic of Kazakhstan
Capital Akmola
Currency Tenge
Main language Kazakh
Population 16.9 million

Kenya
Location East Africa
Official name Republic of Kenya
Capital Nairobi
Currency Kenya shilling
Main languages Swahili and English
Population 29 million

Kiribati
Location Pacific Ocean
Official name Republic of Kiribati
Capital Bairiki, Tarawa Atoll
Currency Australian dollar
Main language English
Population 78,000

Kuwait
Location Middle East
Official name State of Kuwait
Capital Kuwait City
Currency Kuwaiti dinar
Main language Arabic
Population 1.8 million

Kyrgyzstan
Location Central Asia
Official name Kyrgyz Republic
Capital Bishkek
Currency Som
Main language Kyrgyz
Population 4.5 million

Laos
Location Southeast Asia
Official name Lao People's Democratic Republic
Capital Vientiane
Currency New kip
Main language Laotian
Population 5.4 million

Latvia

Location Europe
Official name Republic of Latvia
Capital Riga
Currency Lat
Main language Latvian
Population 2.4 million

Lebanon

Location Middle East
Official name Republic of Lebanon
Capital Beirut
Currency Lebanese pound
Main language Arabic
Population 3.2 million

Lesotho

Location Southern Africa
Official name Kingdom of Lesotho
Capital Maseru
Currency Loti
Main languages English and Sesotho
Population 2.2 million

Liberia

Location West Africa
Official name Republic of Liberia
Capital Monrovia
Currency Liberian dollar
Main language English
Population 2.7 million

Libya

Location North Africa
Official name Great Socialist People's Libyan Arab Jamahariyah
Capital Tripoli/Benghazi
Currency Libyan dinar
Main language Arabic
Population 6 million

Liechtenstein

Location Europe
Official name Principality of Liechtenstein
Capital Vaduz
Currency Swiss franc
Main language German
Population 31,000

Lithuania

Location Europe
Official name Republic of Lithuania
Capital Vilnius
Currency Litas
Main language Lithuanian
Population 3.7 million

Luxembourg

Location Europe
Official name Grand Duchy of Luxembourg
Capital Luxembourg
Currency Euro and Luxembourg franc
Main languages French, German, and Letzebürgisch
Population 422,000

Macedonia

Location Europe
Official name Former Yugoslav Republic of Macedonia
Capital Skopje
Currency Macedonian denar
Main language Macedonian
Population 2.2 million

Madagascar

Location Indian Ocean
Official name Republic of Madagascar
Capital Antananarivo
Currency Franc malagache (Malagasy franc)
Main languages French and Malagasy
Population 16.3 million

Malawi

Location Southern Africa
Official name Republic of Malawi
Capital Lilongwe
Currency Malawi kwacha
Main language English
Population 10.4 million

Malaysia

Location Southeast Asia
Official name Federation of Malaysia
Capital Kuala Lumpur
Currency Ringgit (Malaysian dollar)
Main language English and Bahara Malay
Population 21.5 million

Maldives

Location Indian Ocean
Official name Republic of Maldives
Capital Male
Currency Rufiyaa (Maldivian rupee)
Main language Dhivehi (Maldivian)
Population 282,000

Mali

Location West Africa
Official name Republic of Mali
Capital Bamako
Currency CFA franc
Main language French
Population 11.8 million

Malta

Location Europe
Official name Republic of Malta
Capital Valletta
Currency Maltese lira
Main languages English and Maltese
Population 374,000

Marshall Islands

Location Pacific Ocean
Official name Republic of the Marshall Islands
Capital Delap district, Majuro Atoll
Currency United States dollar
Main languages Marshallese and English
Population 59,000

Mauritania

Location Southern Africa
Official name Islamic Republic of Mauritania
Capital Nouakchott
Currency Ouguiya
Main languages Arabic and French
Population 2.5 million

Mauritius

Location Indian Ocean
Official name Mauritius
Capital Port Louis
Currency Mauritian rupee
Main language English
Population 1.2 million

Mexico

Location Central America
Official name United States of Mexico
Capital Mexico City
Currency Mexican peso
Main language Spanish
Population 95.8 million

The attractive landscape of the Indian Ocean island of Mauritius

Micronesia

Location Pacific Ocean
Official name Federated States of Micronesia
Capital Palikir, Pohnpei island
Currency United States dollar
Main language English
Population 109,000

Moldavia

Location Europe
Official name Republic of Moldova
Capital Chisinau
Currency Leu
Main language Romanian
Population 4.5 million

Monaco

Location Europe
Official name Principality of Monaco
Capital Monaco
Currency French franc
Main language French
Population 32,000

Mongolia

Location Asia
Official name Mongolia
Capital Ulan Bator
Currency Tugrik
Main language Khalkha Mongolian
Population 2.6 million

Morocco

Location North Africa
Official name Kingdom of Morocco
Capital Rabat
Currency Moroccan dirham
Main language Arabic
Population 28 million

Mozambique

Location Southern Africa
Official name Republic of Mozambique
Capital Maputo
Currency Metical
Main language Portuguese
Population 18.7 million

Namibia

Location Southern Africa
Official name Republic of Namibia
Capital Windhoek
Currency Namibian dollar
Main language English
Population 1.7 million

Nauru

Location Pacific Ocean
Official name Republic of Nauru
Capital No official Capital
Currency Australian dollar
Main language Nauruan
Population 11,000

Nepal

Location South Asia
Official name Kingdom of Nepal
Capital Kathmandu
Currency Nepalese rupee
Main language Nepali
Population 23.2 million

Netherlands

Location Europe
Official name Kingdom of the Netherlands
Capital Amsterdam, The Hague
Currency Euro, Netherlands gulden (guilder), and Dutch florin
Main language Dutch
Population 15.7 million

New Zealand

Location Australasia
Official name Dominion of New Zealand
Capital Wellington
Currency New Zealand dollar
Main languages English and Maori
Population 3.7 million

Nicaragua

Location Central America
Official name Republic of Nicaragua
Capital Managua
Currency Córdoba oro
Main language Spanish
Population 4.5 million

Niger

Location West Africa
Official name Republic of Niger
Capital Niamey
Currency CFA franc
Main language French
Population 10.1 million

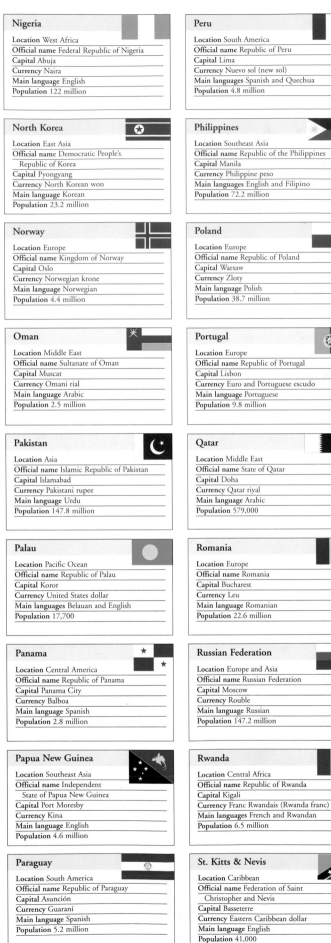

Nigeria
Location West Africa
Official name Federal Republic of Nigeria
Capital Abuja
Currency Naira
Main language English
Population 122 million

North Korea
Location East Asia
Official name Democratic People's Republic of Korea
Capital Pyongyang
Currency North Korean won
Main language Korean
Population 23.2 million

Norway
Location Europe
Official name Kingdom of Norway
Capital Oslo
Currency Norwegian krone
Main language Norwegian
Population 4.4 million

Oman
Location Middle East
Official name Sultanate of Oman
Capital Muscat
Currency Omani rial
Main language Arabic
Population 2.5 million

Pakistan
Location Asia
Official name Islamic Republic of Pakistan
Capital Islamabad
Currency Pakistani rupee
Main language Urdu
Population 147.8 million

Palau
Location Pacific Ocean
Official name Republic of Palau
Capital Koror
Currency United States dollar
Main languages Belauan and English
Population 17,700

Panama
Location Central America
Official name Republic of Panama
Capital Panama City
Currency Balboa
Main language Spanish
Population 2.8 million

Papua New Guinea
Location Southeast Asia
Official name Independent State of Papua New Guinea
Capital Port Moresby
Currency Kina
Main language English
Population 4.6 million

Paraguay
Location South America
Official name Republic of Paraguay
Capital Asunción
Currency Guaraní
Main language Spanish
Population 5.2 million

Peru
Location South America
Official name Republic of Peru
Capital Lima
Currency Nuevo sol (new sol)
Main languages Spanish and Quechua
Population 4.8 million

Philippines
Location Southeast Asia
Official name Republic of the Philippines
Capital Manila
Currency Philippine peso
Main languages English and Filipino
Population 72.2 million

Poland
Location Europe
Official name Republic of Poland
Capital Warsaw
Currency Zloty
Main language Polish
Population 38.7 million

Portugal
Location Europe
Official name Republic of Portugal
Capital Lisbon
Currency Euro and Portuguese escudo
Main language Portuguese
Population 9.8 million

Qatar
Location Middle East
Official name State of Qatar
Capital Doha
Currency Qatar riyal
Main language Arabic
Population 579,000

Romania
Location Europe
Official name Romania
Capital Bucharest
Currency Leu
Main language Romanian
Population 22.6 million

Russian Federation
Location Europe and Asia
Official name Russian Federation
Capital Moscow
Currency Rouble
Main language Russian
Population 147.2 million

Rwanda
Location Central Africa
Official name Republic of Rwanda
Capital Kigali
Currency Franc Rwandais (Rwanda franc)
Main languages French and Rwandan
Population 6.5 million

St. Kitts & Nevis
Location Caribbean
Official name Federation of Saint Christopher and Nevis
Capital Basseterre
Currency Eastern Caribbean dollar
Main language English
Population 41,000

St. Lucia
Location Caribbean
Official name Saint Lucia
Capital Castries
Currency Eastern Caribbean dollar
Main language English
Population 142,000

St. Vincent & the Grenadines
Location Caribbean
Official name Saint Vincent and the Grenadines
Capital Kingstown
Currency Eastern Caribbean dollar
Main language English
Population 111,000

Samoa
Location Pacific Ocean
Official name Independent State of Samoa
Capital Apia
Currency Tala
Main languages English and Samoan
Population 170,000

San Marino
Location Europe
Official name Republic of San Marino
Capital San Marino
Currency Lira
Main language Italian
Population 25,000

São Tomé & Príncipe
Location West Africa
Official name Democratic Republic of São Tomé and Príncipe
Capital São Tomé
Currency Dobra
Main language Portuguese
Population 131,000

Saudi Arabia
Location Middle Easat
Official name Kingdom of Saudi Arabia
Capital Riyadh
Currency Saudi riyal
Main language Arabic
Population 20.2 million

Senegal
Location West Africa
Official name Republic of Senegal
Capital Dakar
Currency CFA franc
Main language French
Population 9 million

Seychelles
Location Indian Ocean
Official name Republic of the Seychelles
Capital Victoria
Currency Seychelles rupee
Main language Seselwa (French Creole)
Population 75,000

Sierra Leone
Location West Africa
Official name Republic of Sierra Leone
Capital Freetown
Currency Leone
Main language English
Population 4.6 million

Singapore
Location Southeast Asia
Official name Republic of Singapore
Capital Singapore
Currency Singapore dollar
Main languages Malay, English, Mandarin Chinese, and Tamil
Population 3.5 million

Slovakia
Location Europe
Official name Slovak Republic
Capital Bratislava
Currency Koruna
Main language Slovak
Population 5.4 million

Slovenia
Location Europe
Official name Republic of Slovenia
Capital Ljubljana
Currency Tolar
Main language Slovene
Population 1.9 million

Solomon Islands
Location Pacific Ocean
Official name Solomon Islands
Capital Honiara
Currency Solomon Islands dollar
Main language English
Population 417,000

Somalia
Location East Africa
Official name Somali Democratic Republic
Capital Mogadishu
Currency Somali shilling
Main language Arabic and Somali
Population 10.7 million

South Africa
Location Southern Africa
Official name Republic of South Africa
Capital Pretoria
Currency Rand
Main languages Afrikaans and English
Population 44.3 million

South Korea
Location East Asia
Official name Republic of Korea
Capital Seoul
Currency South Korean won
Main language Korean
Population 46.1 million

Spain
Location Europe
Official name Kingdom of Spain
Capital Madrid
Currency Euro and Spanish peseta
Main languages Spanish, Galician, Basque, and Catalan
Population 39.8 million

Sri Lanka
Location South Asia
Official name Democratic Socialist Republic of Sri Lanka
Capital Colombo
Currency Sri Lanka rupee
Main languages Sinhala, Tamil, and English
Population 18.5 million

Sudan

Location East Africa
Official name Republic of Sudan
Capital Khartoum
Currency Sudanese pound or dinar
Main language Arabic
Population 28.5 million

Surinam

Location South America
Official name Republic of Surinam
Capital Paramaribo
Currency Surinam gulden (guilder) or florin
Main language Dutch
Population 442,000

Swaziland

Location Southern Africa
Official name Kingdom of Swaziland
Capital Mbabane
Currency Lilangeni
Main languages English and Swazi
Population 931,000

Sweden

Location Europe
Official name Kingdom of Sweden
Capital Stockholm
Currency Swedish krona
Main language Swedish
Population 8.9 million

Switzerland

Location Europe
Official name Swiss Confederation
Capital Berne
Currency Swiss franc
Main languages French, German, and Italian
Population 7.3 million

Syria

Location Middle East
Official name Syrian Arab Republic
Capital Damascus
Currency Syrian pound
Main language Arabic
Population 15.3 million

Taiwan

Location Southeast Asia
Official name Republic of China (Taiwan)
Capital Taipei
Currency Taiwan dollar
Main language Mandarin Chinese
Population 21.5 million

Tajikistan

Location Central Asia
Official name Republic of Tajikistan
Capital Dushanbe
Currency Tajik rouble
Main language Tajik
Population 6.2 million

Tanzania

Location East Africa
Official name United Republic of Tanzania
Capital Dodoma
Currency Tanzanian shilling
Main languages English and Swahili
Population 32.2 million

Istanbul, Turkey, a city on the border between Europe and Asia

Thailand

Location Southeast Asia
Official name Kingdom of Thailand
Capital Bangkok
Currency Baht
Main language Thai
Population 59.6 million

Togo

Location West Africa
Official name Togolese Republic
Capital Lomé
Currency CFA franc
Main language French
Population 4.4 million

Tonga

Location Pacific Ocean
Official name Kingdom of Tonga
Capital Nuku'alofa
Currency Pa'anga (Tongan dollar)
Main languages English and Tongan
Population 97,000

Trinidad & Tobago

Location Caribbean
Official name Republic of Trinidad and Tobago
Capital Port-of-Spain
Currency Trinidad and Tobago dollar
Main language English
Population 1.3 million

Tunisia

Location North Africa
Official name Republic of Tunisia
Capital Tunis
Currency Tunisian dinar
Main language Arabic
Population 9.5 million

Turkey

Location Europe and Asia
Official name Republic of Turkey
Capital Ankara
Currency Turkish lira
Main language Turkish
Population 63.8 million

Turkmenistan

Location Central Asia
Official name Republic of Turkmenistan
Capital Ashgabat
Currency Manat
Main language Turkmen
Population 4.3 million

Tuvalu

Location Pacific Ocean
Official name Tuvalu
Capital Fongafale, Funafuti Atoll
Currency Australian dollar and Tuvaluan dollar
Main language English
Population 10,000

Uganda

Location East Africa
Official name Republic of Uganda
Capital Kampala
Currency New Uganda shilling
Main languages English and Swahili
Population 21.3 million

Ukraine

Location Europe
Official name Ukraine
Capital Kiev
Currency Hryvnia
Main language Ukrainian
Population 51.2 million

United Arab Emirates

Location Middle East
Official name United Arab Emirates
Capital Abu Dhabi
Currency UAE dirham
Main language Arabic
Population 2.4 million

United Kingdom

Location Europe
Official name United Kingdom of Great Britain and Northern Ireland
Capital London
Currency Pound sterling
Main language English
Population 58.2 million

United States

Location North America
Official name United States of America
Capital Washington, D.C.
Currency United States dollar
Main language English
Population 273.8 million

Uruguay

Location South America
Official name Eastern Republic of Uruguay
Capital Montevideo
Currency Uruguayan peso
Main language Spanish
Population 3.2 million

Uzbekistan

Location Central Asia
Official name Republic of Uzbekistan
Capital Tashkent
Currency Som
Main language Uzbek
Population 24.1 million

Vanuatu

Location Pacific Ocean
Official name Republic of Vanuatu
Capital Port-Vila
Currency Vatu
Main languages Bislama, English, and French
Population 200,000

Vatican City

Location Europe
Official name State of the Vatican City
Capital N/A
Currency Lira and Italian lira
Main languages Italian and Latin
Population 1,000

Venezuela

Location South America
Official name Republic of Venezuela
Capital Caracas
Currency Bolivar
Main languages Spanish and Amerindian
Population 23.2 million

Vietnam

Location Southeast Asia
Official name Socialist Republic of Vietnam
Capital Hanoi
Currency Dông
Main language Vietnamese
Population 77.9 million

Yemen

Location Middle East
Official name Republic of Yemen
Capital Sana'a
Currency Rial and dinar
Main language Arabic
Population 16.9 million

Yugoslavia

Location Europe
Official name Federal Republic of Yugoslavia
Capital Belgrade
Currency Yugoslav dinar
Main language Serbo-Croat
Population 10.4 million

Zambia

Location Southern Africa
Official name Republic of Zambia
Capital Lusaka
Currency Zambian kwacha
Main language English
Population 8.7 million

Zimbabwe

Location Southern Africa
Official name Republic of Zimbabwe
Capital Harare
Currency Zimbabwe dollar
Main language English
Population 11.9 million

ENCYCLOPEDIA SUPPLEMENT

APARTHEID

IN 1994 A NEW national flag was flown in South Africa. It symbolized the uniting of all the different races on equal terms for the first time in South African history. In 1948 the inferior status of South Africa's black inhabitants was legalized by a series of discriminatory laws designed to enforce apartheid. Thousands of people were killed or imprisoned for opposing these laws. Although apartheid was abolished in 1991, South Africans are still fighting its poisonous legacy.

What is apartheid?

Apartheid ("separateness" in Afrikaans) is the policy of separate development for people of different races. In 1948, the National Party won control of South Africa, and made apartheid law. Apartheid was an expression of Afrikaner nationalism, but many English-speaking South Africans supported the policy.

The early Dutch tricolour of orange, white, and blue

Flags of Britain, the Orange Free State, and the Transvaal

Old flag of South Africa

The Afrikaners

Afrikaners (Boers) are descendants of the European settlers who lived at the Cape of Good Hope before it became a British colony in 1815. Their independent territories were defeated by the British during the Boer War (1899–1902). Afrikaners speak their own language – a form of Dutch – and practise a Calvinist religion.

Whites and non-whites used separate public facilities, such as toilets.

Apartheid law

The basis of apartheid was the Population Registration Act of 1949, which classed every South African as White, Asian, Coloured (mixed race), or Black. All other apartheid laws stemmed from this basic act of discrimination.

Jobs were allocated according to race.

Apartheid in practice

Apartheid controlled every aspect of daily life. It influenced where and with whom a person lived, and what education that person received. It determined where a person worked and the type of work that could be done. Apartheid governed which shops, cinemas, and swimming pools a person could enter, and it even limited who a person could play sport with. All these different things were subject to the law and were controlled by the government.

Education

The Bantu Education Act of 1953 provided for a separate and lower standard of education for blacks than for whites. Blacks had little chance of improving their education in libraries, as the Reservation of Separate Amenities Act (1953) segregated all public facilities, and there were few black libraries.

Work

Under the Industrial Conciliation Act of 1956, the government reserved jobs for different races and banned the formation of trade unions. Whites held supervisory positions, while blacks were restricted to manual work. The Pass Laws (1958–63) forced black workers to carry pass books at all times – and prevented them from working if they did not.

Townships

The Group Areas Act of 1950 designated parts of the country for different races to live and work. Whites kept the major towns, the best beaches, and the fertile farmlands, while blacks were restricted to poor and barren scrubland. Emptied out of white-only areas, blacks built large squatter camps or townships on the outskirts of major cities. Some, like Soweto, outside Johannesburg, became major cities in their own right.

Some township dwellers live in shacks along unpaved roads.

Township outside Johannesburg

Homelands shown in orange

Homelands

The Bantu Self-Government Act of 1959 established 10 tribal-based homelands that would gradually become politically independent from South Africa. Each black was meant to become a citizen of a homeland, and leave the remainder of South Africa to the white population. Four homelands accepted independence, but none won international recognition. The homelands were poor, overcrowded, and had few resources.

Opposition to apartheid

The South African government kept a tight grip on the country. It used the Suppression of Communism Act (1950) to link anti-apartheid demonstrations with communism. This Act forced protesters to prove their innocence, rather than have the government prove their guilt. During the 1960s and 1970s, protests in the townships and criticism from abroad grew. South Africa became highly disliked and isolated.

International protest
South Africa was constantly criticised at the United Nations, and was forced out of the Commonwealth in 1961. Arms embargoes, trade sanctions, and international boycotts of South African produce harmed the country's economy. South African sportsmen were unable to participate in international sporting events, such as the Olympic games.

Events such as pop concerts promoted the anti-apartheid movement.

The colours of the ANC flag represent people, land, and wealth.

National opposition
Internal opposition to apartheid was led by political organizations, such as the African National Congress, the multi-racial United Democratic Front, and the Zulu-based Inkatha Freedom Party. Some churches and trade unions resisted apartheid, as did several white politicians.

An officer uses a sjambok – *a short whip of dried hide.*

The government's response
The government's reply to any protest was swift and brutal. Black political groups were banned and strong penalties were imposed for breaking the law. The police used spies and secret police to monitor outlawed groups, arrested and detained people without trial, and used torture to extract information. In 1977, the political activist Steve Biko died as a result of injuries received while in police custody.

End of apartheid

International isolation, internal unrest, and economic decline forced the South African government to abandon apartheid. Black organizations were legalized, and apartheid laws were abolished in 1991. The Convention for a Democratic South Africa (CODESA) was set up to draft a new multi-racial constitution. The election of a black president in 1994 ended apartheid permanently.

Reform
Economic decline and a falling white birth-rate meant that a better educated black workforce was required in South Africa. As a result, certain restrictive laws that hindered the economy, including the hated Pass Laws, were abolished after 1985, and closer ties between the races were allowed. The election of F.W. De Klerk as president in 1989 sped up the reform process and led to the complete abolition of all apartheid laws in 1991.

Long queue for the first multi-racial elections

High security fence around a suburban house

After apartheid
Most black people are too ill-educated to get good jobs and too poor to live in South Africa's towns. Industry remains largely white-owned and the best farmland is still white-controlled. High unemployment has increased the level of crime.

Truth and reconciliation
As part of the reform process, President Mandela set up the Truth and Reconciliation Commission in 1995. The committee heard evidence from people on all sides of the racial divide, and uncovered many abuses. Its final report, published in 1998, condemned apartheid as a crime against humanity and found many organisations, including the ANC, guilty of human rights violations.

Timeline

1899–1902 Afrikaners lose their independence during the Boer War.

1910 South Africa becomes independent under English-speaking rule.

1948 The Afrikaner-led National Party wins the South African general election.

1949 The Population Registration Act classifies the population according to race.

1950 Group Areas Act divides the country into racial areas. The Suppression of Communism Act halts all opposition to apartheid.

Separate amenities act, 1953

1961 Fifty-six blacks are killed in the Sharpeville township when police open fire on protestors.

1961 South Africa leaves the Commonwealth and becomes a republic.

1976 Riots occur in Soweto and other townships, in protest at plans to make teaching of Afrikaans compulsory.

1985 Certain apartheid laws are relaxed or abolished.

1986 The United States and the European Community impose economic sanctions on South Africa.

1989 F.W. De Klerk becomes president and begins social reform.

1991 Anti-apartheid groups are legalised and all apartheid laws are abolished.

1994 The first multi-racial elections lead to the election of Nelson Mandela as the president of South Africa.

1998 The Truth and Reconciliation Commission delivers its final report.

FIND OUT MORE   AFRICA, HISTORY OF   GOVERNMENT AND POLITICS   HUMAN RIGHTS   MANDELA, NELSON   SOCIETIES, HUMAN   SOUTH AFRICA   SOUTH AFRICA, HISTORY OF

AUSTRALIAN ENVIRONMENT

THE AUSTRALIAN CONTINENT contains a rich diversity of natural life, including species that cannot be found anywhere else. The indigenous residents – the Aboriginals – had a spiritual bond with their environment that included obligations for its care and protection. Forced off the land by European settlers, the Aboriginals' role in shaping the national parks is gradually being acknowledged, but their fight to reclaim the land continues.

World heritage sites

The protection of parts of Australia began in 1879 with the setting up of the Royal National Park, the world's second-oldest national park. The 1972 World Heritage Convention established the protection of areas with natural or cultural qualities that are of worldwide importance. Australia has 13 World Heritage Sites, including ancient tropical rainforests, unusual landscape features, and areas of Aboriginal culture.

Wet tropics of Queensland

The patches of rainforest on the northeast corner of Australia are all that remains of the tropical forests that once covered most of Australia and Antarctica. These ancient forests are invaluable for their communities of plants, birds, and animals, and contain many marsupial species. The listing of these forests as a World Heritage Site in 1988 removed the severe threat once posed by logging.

Kakadu National Park

The 19,804 sq km (12,306 sq miles) of this park encompass coastlines, rivers, and plateaus. The region contains an extraordinary wealth of species. Aboriginals have occupied the area for more than 25,000 years. Their cave paintings made the site famous.

Shark Bay is covered with stromatolites, which are made up of the oldest known forms of life.

Uluru-Kata Tjuta National Park contains the world's largest monolith – Uluru (Ayers Rock).

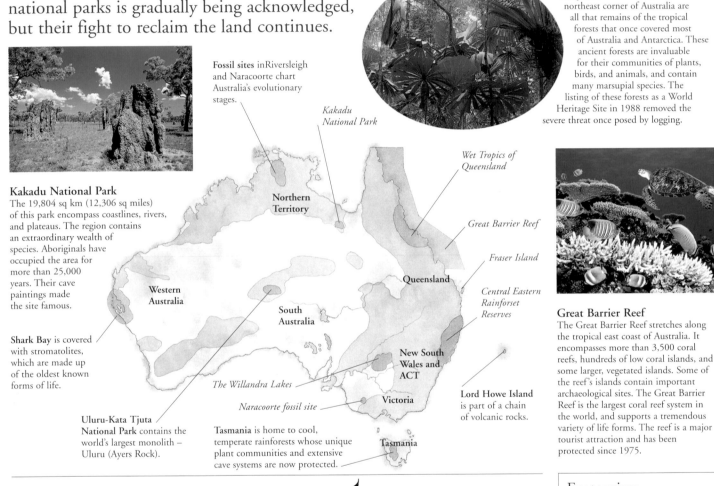

Fossil sites in Riversleigh and Naracoorte chart Australia's evolutionary stages.

Kakadu National Park

Wet Tropics of Queensland

Northern Territory

Western Australia

South Australia

Queensland

Great Barrier Reef

Fraser Island

Central Eastern Rainforset Reserves

New South Wales and ACT

The Willandra Lakes

Naracoorte fossil site

Victoria

Lord Howe Island is part of a chain of volcanic rocks.

Tasmania is home to cool, temperate rainforests whose unique plant communities and extensive cave systems are now protected.

Tasmania

Great Barrier Reef

The Great Barrier Reef stretches along the tropical east coast of Australia. It encompasses more than 3,500 coral reefs, hundreds of low coral islands, and some larger, vegetated islands. Some of the reef's islands contain important archaeological sites. The Great Barrier Reef is the largest coral reef system in the world, and supports a tremendous variety of life forms. The reef is a major tourist attraction and has been protected since 1975.

Land ownership

When Europeans first colonised Australia, they declared the land *terra nullius*, which meant that the land belonged to no-one and was free to be claimed by the settlers. The human rights of the Aboriginals were ignored, but the federal government is now trying to improve conditions for them. Authority over land use lies with each of Australia's seven states, but government initiatives have provided money for an indigenous land fund and a federal social justice package.

1993 Native Title Legislation

Aboriginals and those supporting their interests have long lobbied for changes in the law that would enable them to establish legal rights and ownership over lands that are theirs by tradition. The Native Title Act of 1993 went some way towards achieving this aim, but it does not allow Aboriginals to have actual control over land, even if it lies within the borders of a protected area. Attempts by the Australian High Court to interpret this legislation added further complications, and the controversy over native land rights continues.

Ecotourism

Tourism is an important part of the economy of the Great Barrier Reef, but large numbers of tourists cause problems. Today, the government encourages tourism that is sustainable and not harmful to the environment. The reef has been divided into zones to protect it, and areas with sensitive ecosystems are closed to tourists.

FIND OUT MORE

ABORIGINAL AUSTRALIANS   AUSTRALIA   AUSTRALIA, HISTORY OF   BURKE AND WILLS

BURKE AND WILLS

THE FIRST EUROPEANS in Australia settled around the coastline and rarely ventured inland. In the 1850s, the centre of Australia was still largely unknown. In 1859 the South Australia government offered a prize to the first person who could cross the continent from south to north. Robert Burke took up the challenge.

Expedition leaders

The impulsive and fiery Robert Burke led an expedition of 18 men, 24 camels, and 28 horses. They carried 21 tons of provisions, which included rum for the camels and brandy for the men. The camels were chosen for their ability to travel on stony ground for days, without water. They were imported from Asia, and had three Indian drivers to tend them.

Robert O'Hara Burke
Born in County Galway, Ireland, Robert Burke (1821–61) joined the Austro-Hungarian army before emigrating to Australia, where he became the district inspector of police. Burke lacked the qualities required in an expedition leader. He was bad at planning and had no experience of the outback.

Expedition route
The expedition left Melbourne on 21 August 1860. From Menindee, six members continued to Cooper's Creek. In December, four of them continued to the Gulf of Carpentaria, arriving in February 1861. The party returned to Cooper's Creek on 21 April 1861.

William John Wills
Born in Devonshire, England, William Wills (1834–61) trained as a surveyor. His knowledge of astronomy and his experience of the outback helped him to make his careful field notes. At the age of 26, Wills was too young and inexperienced to stand up to Burke. He became the second-in-command midway through the journey.

Expedition

The expedition was sponsored by the Royal Society of Victoria and had a grand start. The group paraded through the streets of Melbourne before heading north. The trip was poorly planned, and this led to the deaths of its leaders. Despite its tragic ending, the expedition was a success of sorts, for it proved that it was possible to cross Australia overland from south to north. Burke and Wills's destination was unsuitable for settlement, however – the Gulf of Carpentaria is marshy and inhospitable, and remains largely uninhabited to this day.

Keeping a record
Wills kept a log of each day's events. Both Wills and Ludwig Becker, a German naturalist, made records of the flora, fauna, and landscape that they observed. Their notes proved invaluable for later surveying expeditions.

Cooper's Creek
The main camp was pitched at Cooper's Creek, a river in the Sturt Desert. From there, four men – Burke, Wills, Gray, and King – set off on foot for the Gulf of Carpentaria, leaving a few men behind. On their return four months later, the weary travellers discovered that the support party had left earlier the same day, leaving a few provisions at the camp. After two months spent wandering in the bush, trying to find a route home, Burke and Wills died of starvation. A search party found King living with an Aboriginal community.

Memorial stone at Cooper's Creek

Fatal errors
The expedition was fatally flawed from the very start. There were too many men for the party to move quickly through the inhospitable terrain. They carried too many supplies, and this slowed them down. The camels were unsuited to the conditions and, in the end, most of them were eaten for food. Most crucially, Burke was a poor leader, and in his impatience to reach the Gulf of Carpentaria, he chose to leave behind vital food supplies, which the expedition would later require. Today, the descendants of the camels that survived the exhibition live wild in the outback.

Opening up Australia
The exploration work of the numerous rescue parties that searched for Burke and Wills opened up the Australian interior. The pressure to find new land suitable for grazing cattle meant that many farmers were willing to move into the interior. Soon after Burke and Wills's expedition ended, farmers from the eastern coast started crossing the Great Dividing Range and settling in the vast pastures of the outback.

A sheep station in the Australian interior

FIND OUT MORE   ABORIGINAL AUSTRALIANS   AUSTRALIA   AUSTRALIA, HISTORY OF   AUSTRALIAN WILDLIFE   EXPLORERS

CHURCHILL, WINSTON

"THE GREATEST ENGLISHMAN of our time" was how one politician described Winston Churchill, the man who led Britain to victory in World War II. Churchill had immense ability, great energy, and a gift for oratory. He became prime minister when Britain faced defeat in 1940, having "nothing to offer but blood, toil, tears, and sweat".

Blenheim Palace

Early life
Winston Churchill was born in 1874 at Blenheim Palace, Oxfordshire. His father Randolph was a prominent Conservative politician. The young Churchill served in the army and later worked as a war correspondent.

World War I
In 1911, Churchill was appointed First Lord of the Admiralty to prepare the navy for possible war against Germany. Following the failed 1915 Dardanelles campaign, he resigned from the government and went to fight on the Western Front. He returned to government in 1917 as minister of munitions, and was made secretary of state for war and for air in 1919.

Early career
Churchill's early political career was erratic and only partially successful. As the Conservative government's Chancellor of the Exchequer (1924–29), he tied the British currency to a high exchange rate. This caused mass unemployment and recession. His opposition to Indian home rule further isolated him. By the mid-1930s, his political career appeared to be over.

Into office
In 1900, Churchill was elected to Parliament as a Conservative. He defected to the Liberals in 1904 because of their support for free trade. Churchill became Home Secretary in 1910, and was viewed as a reformist minister with firm views on law and order. He lost his seat in the general election of 1922.

With his wife Clementine

World War II
At the outbreak of war in 1939, Churchill was recalled to government in his old post of First Lord of the Admiralty. He was an energetic and popular minister, and was the ideal choice to become prime minister when Neville Chamberlain resigned in 1940. As head of an all-party coalition government, Churchill mobilized all available resources to fight a total war against Germany, Japan, and Italy.

Inspirational leader
Throughout the war, Churchill toured the country, inspecting the war effort and raising morale. He was a fine orator, inspiring Britain to believe it could defeat Germany even in the darkest days of the war when invasion seemed imminent. His personal symbol – the reversed-finger V-sign – represented his confidence in victory.

War strategy
As prime minister, Churchill devised a war strategy with the USA and the USSR to defeat Germany through air dominance and a land invasion of western Europe. He stepped up aircraft production and authorized nightly bombing raids on German cities and military targets.

Cabinet War Rooms

After the war
In 1945, the Conservatives were unexpectedly defeated by the Labour Party and Churchill became the leader of the opposition. He remained an important politician, and voiced concern about the Soviet domination of Eastern Europe. In a speech given in 1946, he warned that an "iron curtain" was threatening to divide Europe into communist east and capitalist west.

Back in power
In 1951, the Conservatives won the general election. At the age of 77, Churchill became prime minister for the second time. His government did much to rebuild the British economy, which had been devastated by the war. In 1953, Churchill was made a Knight of the Garter.

Garter Star

Goldfish at Chartwell

Later life
After his retirement as prime minister in 1955, Churchill remained an MP until 1964, although he took little part in active political life. After further illness, he died in January 1965, at the age of 90. His state funeral was attended by heads of government and of state from all over the world.

Other interests
Throughout his life Churchill pursued interests outside politics. He was a skilled artist, and wrote many books of history and biography at Chartwell, his country retreat. He was awarded the Nobel Prize for Literature in 1953.

WINSTON CHURCHILL
1874	Born in Blenheim Palace.
1900	Enters Parliament as a Conservative.
1904	Defects to the Liberal Party.
1940	Becomes prime minister of the wartime government.
1951	Becomes prime minister for the second time.
1953	Awarded knighthood and the Nobel Prize for Literature.
1955	Retires as prime minister.
1964	Leaves Parliament.
1965	Dies, aged 90.

FIND OUT MORE — EUROPE, HISTORY OF; UNITED KINGDOM, HISTORY OF; WORLD WAR II

ENGLAND

ENGLAND IS AT THE CENTRE of the United Kingdom in more ways than one. Thanks to its capital, London, it is the trading and administrative centre of the UK – until recently, other UK nations were also governed from London. England's power has declined since the days of the British Empire, but this small, overcrowded country is still an important force in world politics.

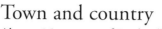

The region
England, the largest nation in the UK, occupies the middle and most of the south of mainland Britain. Much of the countryside is flat, especially in the south and east, but there are mountain ranges in the northwest, and the scenery of the Lake District is particularly beautiful.

Leisure

Sport is an important part of English culture. Many people take part in amateur sports, while even more are keen spectators. Other favourite English pastimes include gardening, visiting the theatre or cinema, and shopping.

Sport
Football is the most popular sport in England – 20 million fans follow the football season from August to May. Rugby Union has a large following, and Rugby League is especially popular in northern England. Cricket is played in many villages and towns during the summer. Shooting, fishing, and hunting are important country sports.

Dame Judi Dench in Shakespeare in Love

Film industry
The English film industry flourished in the 1950s, but was in decline until recently. Many English directors, writers, and actors still find international success, however – such as Anthony Minghella, Ralph Fiennes, and Dame Judi Dench.

Entertainment
English social life centres around the local pub, especially in the villages. People meet to drink beer, talk, and play pub sports such as darts. Many people enjoy eating out at restaurants and cafes. To keep fit, the English jog, walk, or attend fitness classes or a gym.

Town and country

Almost 95 per cent of England's population live in cities or towns – 40 per cent are crammed into the seven largest cities. The 1990s have seen many people move to country villages in search of a better quality of life. Today, rural populations are growing more quickly than urban ones, and this is putting pressure on the countryside.

Kingfishers are one bird species threatened by the decline in waterways.

Vanishing countryside
Urbanization has devastated much of the English countryside. Industrial and housing developments have, for example, destroyed almost half of British rivers, threatening the rich diversity of wildlife. Many sites of historical interest have also disappeared.

Royal family
The English monarch Elizabeth II is head of state, but her role is ceremonial and she has little real power. Recently, after a number of scandals, the popularity of the royal family has declined. The royals have since worked hard to improve their "stuffy" image.

Population
England has a multi-cultural society. Since the 1950s, more than two million people have emigrated to Britain, many coming from its former colonies. England, especially, has reaped the rich benefits of an ethnic mix of people, but there has been racial conflict, too – especially in the inner cities.

Urbanization
The spread of towns into the countryside is a major environmental issue facing England. The government predicts that 4.4 million extra homes will be needed by 2016. Rather than regenerating inner cities, they are allowing developers to turn an area of rural land the size of London into towns.

London

The largest city in Europe, London is steeped in history. The city has been the heart of English government, and an international centre of business and trade for 1,000 years. It is still one of the world's major financial centres. London is also one of the cultural centres of England, with many notable art galleries, theatres, museums, and churches.

Bank of England

FIND OUT MORE   EUROPE   EUROPE, HISTORY OF   EUROPEAN WILDLIFE   UNITED KINGDOM

GULF WAR

IN 1990 IRAQ INVADED KUWAIT to gain possession of Kuwait's massive oil reserves. An international coalition of 28 nations assembled to liberate Kuwait. The war that resulted was the most technologically advanced war in recent history. The allied forces used sophisticated weaponry and military intelligence to achieve victory after just 100 hours of ground fighting. The threat that Iraq could use biological, chemical, or nuclear weapons made the conflict extremely dangerous.

Iraqi targets

Israel Iraq *Allied targets*

Saudi Arabia Kuwait

Gulf region

Most of the world's oil reserves are located around or beneath the Persian Gulf. This makes it one of the most important and strategic waterways in the world. Iraq is sandwiched between Iran, Kuwait, and Saudi Arabia. Control of Kuwait would allow Iraq to dominate the Persian Gulf.

Iraqi forces

Iraq was almost completely isolated, with the support of only Jordan and a few Arab states, none of whom supplied troops. The 545,000-strong Iraqi army was led by the elite Republican Guard, and included 1,850 tanks and 500 aircraft. They threatened to fight, in Saddam Hussein's words, "the mother of all battles".

Iraqi leader Saddam Hussein

Operation Desert Storm

At midnight on 16 January 1991 – one day after the UN deadline for Iraq to leave Kuwait – coalition planes bombarded Baghdad, the Iraqi capital. A month later, on 24 February, troops launched a ground offensive to liberate Kuwait. This objective was achieved on 28 February, after 100 hours of fighting, when Iraq accepted a provisional ceasefire.

Coalition soldiers

Weapons of war

The coalition used lasers and computers to guide bombs and cruise missiles. Their F-117 Stealth fighter evaded enemy radar. The Iraqis used the Soviet-made Scud missile system to attack both Saudi Arabia and Israel, although the system was destroyed before it could fire chemical or biological warheads.

Coalition forces

The main participants were the USA, Britain, and France, plus a group of Arab countries opposed to Iraq, led by Saudi Arabia, Syria, and Egypt. The total coalition forces – led by US General Norman Schwarzkopf – numbered 700,000 troops, with 2,200 combat aircraft and 530 attack helicopters.

Soldiers carry a missile

Aftermath

The consequences of the war were immense. Kuwait City and Baghdad suffered considerable damage from bombing. More than 33,000 Kuwaitis were killed or captured by the Iraqis, who lost between 85,000 and 100,000 soldiers and an unknown number of civilians. Only 234 coalition troops lost their lives, many to "friendly fire" from their own side.

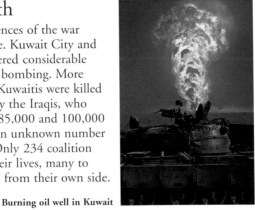

Burning oil well in Kuwait

Cost of war

The Iraqis deliberately released crude oil into the Persian Gulf to prevent an amphibious landing in Kuwait. As they withdrew from Kuwait, the Iraqis set fire to more than 700 oil wells. These actions caused immense environmental damage to the region.

Political effects

The war left Iraq isolated in the Arab world. Continued international sanctions, and air raids by the USA and Britain to force Iraq to disarm, have led to a weakening of the international coalition. Many Arab states now feel greater sympathy toward Iraq.

Gulf War syndrome

After the war, some coalition veterans developed a range of ailments. The troops might have been poisoned either by Iraqi chemical weapons or by the drugs given to them as a defence against chemical or biological attack.

Antidotes for nerve gas attacks

Timeline

1961 Kuwait gains independence from Britain and is claimed by Iraq.

1979 Saddam Hussein becomes leader of Iraq and introduces repressive rule.

July 1990 Talks over Iraq's claim to Kuwait break down.

2 August 1990 Iraq invades Kuwait and holds westerners as hostages.

29 November 1990 UN authorizes its members to use all means to secure the liberation of Kuwait.

16 January 1991 Air bombardment of Iraq begins.

18 January 1991 Iraqis begin to fire Scud missiles into Israel.

Aftermath of Iraqi bombs

24 January 1991 Allied seaborne assault on a Kuwaiti island in the Gulf.

24 February 1991 Allied forces enter Kuwait and begin the ground war.

28 February 1991 Kuwait is liberated after Iraq accepts a provisional ceasefire.

12 April 1991 Definitive ceasefire takes effect.

FIND OUT MORE GULF STATES IRAN AND IRAQ OIL UNITED NATIONS UNITED STATES, HISTORY OF WARFARE WEAPONS

INDIAN ARCHITECTURE

TEMPLES, TOMBS, palaces, and forts dot the Indian landscape. Ancient texts, such as the *Shilpa Shastra*, laid down the basics of Hindu architecture. Foreign invaders, colonizers, and traders enriched this architectural tradition by importing their own cultural styles. During the British Raj, European building techniques led to Indo-Saracenic architecture.

Early Indian architecture
One of the earliest forms of Indian architecture is the Buddhist stupa, which symbolizes a cosmic wheel. Early Hindu masons not only built from wood and stone, but also carved temples into the living rock, such as those found at Ellora in Maharashtra.

Buddhist stupa at Sanchi

Medieval architecture

From the 11th century onwards, northern India came under the power of Mongol and Afghan invaders who introduced Islamic architecture into the region. Hindu kingdoms flourished in the south, where temple architecture evolved a style with towering entrance gateways called *gopurams*.

Verses from the Qu'ran are elaborately carved on the tower.

Qutb Minar
This monumental tower was erected by Qutbuddin Aibak – the first sultan of the Slave dynasty. Standing 72.5 m (238 ft) high, it was, for centuries, the highest freestanding structure in India. It is made of red sandstone and is carved with texts from the Qu'ran.

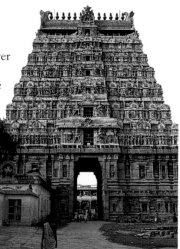

Nataraja Temple,
The Nataraja Temple in Chidambaram, Tamil Nadu, was built in the 12th or 13th century during the Chola dynasty. It is dedicated to Lord Shiva in the form of Nataraja, the cosmic dancer. The temple has the largest and most elaborate gateways in southern India from this period, which are impressive examples of the Chola style.

Mughal architecture

Mughal architecture represents one of the richest and most creative styles in India. The Mughals enhanced the Indo-Islamic style with added decorative and ornamental flourishes. Gold, silver, and precious stones were lavishly used, and marble became the preferred building material.

Fatehpur Sikri
In 1570, the emperor Akbar established a new capital on the outskirts of Agra. The city of Fatehpur Sikri was built in less than ten years, abandoned after fourteen, and still exists in a remarkable state of preservation.

Dome 87 m (285 ft) high

Taj Mahal
The Taj Mahal is considered to be one of the most elegant and harmonious buildings in the world. Built by Mughal emperor Shah Jahan as a monument for his beloved wife, Mumtaz Mahal, each aspect of the Taj represents complex Islamic cosmological concepts.

White marble with pietra dura inlay

Colonial architecture

The British brought new architectural features, such as palladian frontages, Ionic columns, and stately porticos, into India in the 18th and early 19th centuries. In the mid-19th century, the popular Victorian Gothic style was imported, mixed with Indian decorative elements, and the crenellated and kiosked results are visible across the country.

Old Delhi Secretariat Complex

Neoclassical
Corinthian and Ionic columns proliferated during the colonial period, and the character of towns changed to reflect the might of British rule. The order and elegance of neoclassical buildings, such as Delhi's secretariat complex, was viewed as superior to what the British dismissed as the "tangle" of Hindu architecture.

Victoria Terminus
This railway station was built by F. W. Stevens as the Bombay headquarters for the Great India Peninsular Railway. Opened in 1887 to celebrate Queen Victoria's Golden Jubilee, it is a magnificent building, blending Venetian, Gothic, and Indo-Saracenic styles, with gothic arches, spires, and monkey-gargoyles, topped by the allegorical figure of Progress.

Bungalows

The bungalow is a legacy of the Raj, originally designed to house single white men living in remote outposts. It was built of brick and covered with *chuna*, a substance made of crushed sea shells and lime. Shaded interiors made bungalows so popular that they displaced the traditional *havelis*.

FIND OUT MORE   ARCHITECTURE   INDIA   INDIA, HISTORY OF

INDIAN CINEMA

An actor portrays Ganesh, the elephant-headed god.

SINCE THE MAKING OF the first feature film in 1913, the Indian film industry has grown to be the largest in the world. Almost 900 films are released every year, and more than 23 million Indians visit the cinema daily. The main types of Indian film are popular cinema – also called "Bollywood" or "masala" movies – mythological dramas based on religious stories, and art cinema. A number of western films have been set in India.

Masala movies

Romantic leads, wicked villains, comedy, fights, and lavish sets are ingredients that add *masala* (spice) to an Indian popular film. The more successful movies are unashamedly escapist, and simply aim to provide entertainment. Musical routines form the core of these productions and fuel the huge popular music industry.

Poster of Jayalalitha on a street in Madras (Chennai)

Stars

Indian movie stars are among the highest-paid and the most famous people in India. Amitabh Bachchan was India's biggest superstar for nearly two decades. Today, the most popular heroes include Shah Rukh Khan and Aamir Khan, while Madhuri Dixit and Manisha Koirala are popular heroines. Some powerful politicians, such as Jayalalitha, started their careers as film stars.

Mythologicals

Mythological films bring Hindu epics such as the *Mahabharata* and the *Ramayana* to life. The special effects may seem amateurish today, but past masters like Babubhai Mistri have enthralled audiences since the 1930s. The actors who play the parts of gods and goddesses are often treated like deities by their fans.

Cameraman films a scene.

Making movies

As in Hollywood, India's tinsel town, Bombay – or Bollywood, as it is often called – is a magnet for movie moguls, glamorous stars, and struggling actors. Important directors, such as Yash Chopra, Subhash Ghai, and Mani Ratnam, can command a budget of over £2 million, although some popular films have been made for as little as £11,000.

Art cinema

Art cinema constitutes only ten per cent of the Indian film industry. This genre differs from popular cinema in theme, style, and content. Serious film-makers, such as Satyajit Ray, Ritwik Ghatak, and Govind Nihalani, have made bold films dealing with real social and political issues. Their films have received critical acclaim at international film festivals in London, Paris, Cannes, and Berlin.

Still from the film *Fire* (1998)

Feminism in art cinema

Indian women film-makers, such as Aparna Sen and Deepa Mehta, now play an important role in the industry. Highly acclaimed, yet controversial films like Sen's *Paroma* and Mehta's *Fire* explore themes of female identity and sexuality in a male-dominated world.

Lake District scenery

On location

Most Bollywood films are shot in or near Bombay, but song and dance sequences often use picturesque European locations. Switzerland is popular, but much of the hit movie *Dilwale Dulhanya Le Jayenge* was shot in the Lake District, UK.

Satyajit Ray

Satyajit Ray (1921–92) is India's most famous art film director. His first film was the classic *Pather Panchali* (1955). Ray's films were noted for their realism, and for their moving and subtle depiction of village life. He also wrote original screenplays, film scores, adaptations, and children's stories. In 1992, Satyajit Ray received an Oscar for his work.

| FIND OUT MORE | FILMS AND FILMMAKING | INDIA AND SRI LANKA | INDIA, HISTORY OF | MYTHS AND LEGENDS |

INDIAN FESTIVALS

INDIA'S MANY DIFFERENT religious communities have their own festivals. Celebrations mark the passage between birth, death, and renewal. Particular rituals, dress, food, dances, and songs are associated with each special day. Festival days are set not according to the linear calendar, but by the lunar cycle and the changing seasons.

Baisakhi
In Punjab and Haryana, Baisakhi marks the new year and the harvest of the winter crop. It is important to Sikhs as it coincides with the anniversary of the founding of the Khalsa. Men dance the energetic *bhangra*, while women dance the *gidda*.

Colourful dyes show up well on white clothes.

Children playing holi

Spring festivals
Spring festivals take place from mid-January until early April, when seeds for the new crops are sown. Celebrations mark the farewell to winter, which can be particularly severe in northern India. Prayers are offered for a good harvest.

Holi
During the spring festival of Holi, people throw powdered paints and water of every hue at each other. There is a carnival air, with much dancing and singing on the streets and in people's homes. The celebration cuts through caste, gender, and other social barriers.

Powders used during Holi

Vasant Panchami
This Hindu festival marks the start of spring. People wear bright yellow clothes to mirror the mustard flowers that are in bloom. Vasant Panchami originated as a fertility rite. It continues to be important among farmers.

Monsoon festivals
The monsoon brings an end to the searing heat of summer in June, and continues until early September. It is a time of great celebration across the country to welcome the rains and the onset of the cool weather.

Diwali
The festival of lights, Diwali is celebrated all over India. It is associated with Lakshmi, the goddess of wealth, who is welcomed into homes by lighting *diyas* (small clay lamps). Diwali is a time of great rejoicing, marked by setting off fireworks and the exchange of sweets among relatives and friends.

Raksha Bandhan
Raksha Bandhan is a touching ceremony in which sisters tie brightly coloured bands called *rakhis* around the wrists of their brothers as a symbol of protection and love. The streets are full of little stalls selling *rakhis* in all types of colourful designs, from the simple to the wonderfully elaborate.

Janmashtami
This August festival celebrates the birth of the Hindu god Krishna. Houses are decorated with small footprints, to symbolise the child Krishna entering the home. Worshippers also undertake symbolic fasting.

Teej
Celebrated in northern India, Teej is a monsoon festival dedicated to the goddess Parvati. Women dress in brightly coloured clothes and decorate their palms with elaborate henna designs. They sit in swings that are hung from the branches of mango and peepul trees, and sing to welcome the rains.

Music and dance
Dance and song are an integral part of most Indian festivals. The colourful and vivacious *bhangra* dance of Punjabis celebrating Baisakhi is accompanied by rhythmic drumming. At Diwali, young girls holding lighted butter-lamps will often join in elegant, swirling dances.

Sweets piled up in offering to the Hindu gods Rama, Lakshmi, and Sita.

Festival foods
Every festival has its own unique regional foods, but sweets are common to all. During festival time, the sweet shops are full of people buying *barfis*, *laddus*, *gulab jamuns*, and other sweets. Indian sweets are made with milk, curd, nuts, sugar, and date syrup.

FIND OUT MORE | CLOTHES AND FASHION | FESTIVALS | HINDUISM | INDIA AND SRI LANKA | INDIA, HISTORY OF | RELIGIONS | SIGNS AND SYMBOLS

INDIAN WILDLIFE

INDIA IS HOME to some of the world's most beautiful, and dangerous, creatures, such as the cobra and the tiger. The different climatic zones within the subcontinent allow a wide variety of wildlife to thrive, including more than 350 mammal species, 2,000 bird, and 500 reptile species, as well as countless forms of insect and marine life. Plant life is also abundant.

Delicate ecosystems

India's delicate ecosystem is under threat from industrialization, pollution, and loss of natural habitat to farming, as well as hunting and poaching. Under the Wildlife Act, passed by Parliament in 1972, more than 330 wildlife sanctuaries and 66 national parks have been established.

Conservation
There is grave concern that many of India's endangered species, such as the Asiatic lion and the Indian rhinoceros, may become extinct. Government schemes, such as Project Tiger, and grassroots initiatives, like the Chipko tree conservation movement, have helped raise awareness about vital environmental issues.

Natural habitats
The sub-Himalayan region of northern India is covered with Indian pine, teak, peepul, and eucalyptus forests. This area is also home to monkeys, elephants, jungle cats, and deer. India's largest deer, the sambhar, is found in the arid and semi-arid deciduous forests. Marshes and mangrove swamps are favourite stopping points for migratory and resident birds.

Climatic zones
The landmass making up the Indian subcontinent contains many different climatic zones – from tropical jungles to temperate deciduous forests, palm-fringed coasts to lush mangrove swamps, the deserts of Rajasthan to the icy peaks of the Himalayas.

- Tropical rainforest
- Monsoon forest
- Dry tropical scrub
- Dry tropical forest
- Desert
- Mountain vegetation

National parks

India is home to more than 400 national parks and wildlife sanctuaries, providing a haven for many threatened species of flora and fauna. The 1,597 sq km (617 sq mile) Helghat Tiger Reserve, Maharashtra, is the largest park in the country, while Ranganathittu bird sanctuary in Karnataka is the smallest, at just 1 sq km (0.4 sq mile).

Animal kingdom

In India, animals play an important part in people's everyday lives, even in the cities. The water-buffalo is used to pull heavy loads and plough fields. The cow is revered by Hindus as a sacred animal, as are elephants and some snakes.

Indian elephant
In India, tame elephants have been used by people for thousands of years, to lift and transport heavy loads, and in ceremonies, battles, and processions. Indian elephants have several noticeable differences from their African cousins – they are slightly smaller, have smaller ears, and the females do not grow tusks. They can live for up to 80 years.

Peacock
The peacock is a royal bird, frequently shown in paintings strolling on the lawns of a maharaja's palace. The male has dramatic tail feathers of turquoise, green, and gold, which he fans in a shimmering display during courtship and territorial dances. Under British rule, peacocks were frequently shipped back to the gardens of English country houses.

Bharatpur Sanctuary, Rajasthan

Cobra
The most celebrated and worshipped snake in the world is the cobra. It is one of four common poisonous snakes in India, and displays a beautiful hood when disturbed. The king cobra can grow up to 5 m (16 ft) in length and is generally found in deep jungles with mild, humid climates. In South India, a corner of each home is dedicated to the sacred cobra.

Cobra shows hood when disturbed.

King Cobra

Indian tiger
One of the most magnificent animals in the cat family, the Indian tiger is the national animal of India, and a protected species. Tiger hunts were a popular pastime for the British colonialists and Indian royalty. Even though hunting is now banned, the continued destruction of natural habitats has led to tiger populations in India dwindling from an estimated 40,000 to just over 4,000 in less than 60 years.

Animals in mythology
One of the best-loved gods in Hinduism is elephant-headed Ganesh. His father, Shiva, is frequently depicted with a king cobra, while Durga, the demon-slayer mother goddess, is often shown riding a lion. Hanuman, the monkey-god, is renowned for his strength and agility, and his devoted service to Lord Rama.

Goddess Durga killing the buffalo-demon Mahisasura

FIND OUT MORE — ANIMALS · ECOLOGY AND ECOSYSTEMS · INDIA AND SRI LANKA · RAINFOREST WILDLIFE

LEWIS AND CLARK

IN 1783, MOST AMERICANS lived in a thin strip of land along the Atlantic coast. The rest of the continent remained largely unexplored. In 1803 President Thomas Jefferson bought from France the Louisiana Territory, a vast tract of land west of the Mississippi River. Jefferson sent an expedition, led by Meriwether Lewis and William Clark, to map this new acquisition and report back on everything they saw.

Return route

Return route

Rocky Mountains

Outward journey

Mississippi River

Expedition routes
Lewis and Clark left St. Louis in May 1804. They paddled up the Missouri River, crossed the Rockies, and travelled down the Columbia River, reaching the Pacific in December 1805. On the return journey, Lewis and Clark took separate routes across the Rockies, before reuniting and returning to St. Louis in 1806.

William Clark (1770–1838) served in the army until his resignation in 1796. He travelled widely until 1803, when he received a letter from his friend Lewis, inviting him to join the expedition.

Meriwether Lewis (1774–1809) was the organizer and co-leader of the expedition. In his youth, Lewis fought in the army's campaigns against the Native Americans of the Great Lakes region. In 1801, he became personal secretary to President Jefferson.

Expedition leaders

The Corps of Discovery – as the expedition was officially known – was led by Meriwether Lewis and William Clark. They were assisted by a team of 45 woodsmen and hunters, some of whom were former soldiers, chosen for their ability to survive in the wild. The expedition was joined by a Native American woman, Sagajawea, through whose Shoshone tribal lands they passed.

Sagajawea ("Bird woman") joined the expedition while the Corps camped at the Mandan villages, during the winter of 1804. She could speak many local languages, and became the expedition's interpreter. Sagajawea arranged for her Shoshone tribe to provide a guide and horses to help the Corps across the Rocky Mountains.

Native Americans presented this painted buffalo skin to Lewis and Clark.

Expedition

Lewis and Clark travelled a total of 12,000 km (7,500 miles), and took more than two years to cross the American continent from the Midwest to the Pacific coast and back again. They survived two winters in forts that they had built themselves. The only expedition member who did not return safely died of a ruptured appendix.

.45 Colt Peacemaker

Broad brim shades the eyes and neck.

Stetson hat

Native Americans
The territory the expedition travelled through was inhabited by Native American peoples, such as the Mandan, Shoshone, Blackfoot, and Sioux. Some of these tribes provided guides and provisions, and helped the expedition to cross mountainous and inhospitable terrain. At night, Lewis and Clark would entertain their hosts with violin music and tobacco.

Lewis noted the appearance, size, smell, and even taste of the many plants he found.

Natural history
President Jefferson instructed Lewis to "study the soil and face of the country", and to record the weather and any volcanic activity. Lewis took his job seriously, and kept detailed notes of everything that he saw. He shipped back numerous plant and animal specimens for scientific examination.

SHERIFF

Sheriff's badge

Westward expansion
The success of the expedition convinced the US government that the West was suitable for settlement. In 1845, journalist John O'Sullivan wrote that the United States had a "manifest destiny" to expand its frontiers across the entire continent. Within a few years, settlers were pouring westwards to start a new life on the Great Plains and the Pacific coastline.

FIND OUT MORE   EXPLORATION   NATIVE AMERICANS   NORTH AMERICA   NORTH AMERICA, HISTORY OF   NORTH AMERICAN WILDLIFE   UNITED STATES, HISTORY OF

LINCOLN, ABRAHAM

ONE OF THE MOST FAMOUS presidents in US history, Abraham Lincoln was disliked during his term of office. When he was elected president in 1860, less than half the country supported him and 11 states left the Union in protest against his anti-slavery views. As a war leader, he struggled to keep the Union together. He inspired many people with his speeches on freedom, and in 1865, led the Union to victory in the Civil War.

Lincoln's birthplace, Kentucky, USA

Humble beginnings

Lincoln was born in poverty in a log cabin in Hardin County, Kentucky in 1809. He moved with his parents to Indiana in 1816 and then to Illinois, where he worked in a store in New Salem. In 1833 he began to study law, paying for his studies by working as a postmaster. He qualified as a lawyer in 1836.

The political man

In 1834 Lincoln won election to the Illinois state legislature, where he remained for eight years. He entered national politics in 1847 when he was elected to the House of Representatives, but failed to win re-election and retired in 1849, returning to law.

The issue of slavery

The ownership of slaves was common across southern USA but the northern states were fiercely against it. Lincoln opposed any extension of slavery to the new western states joining the Union, and in 1858 he re-entered national politics to challenge Stephen Douglas, the sitting, pro-extension Democratic senator for Illinois. Although he did not win, he made a national reputation for himself.

Standing for president

In 1860 Lincoln won the nomination of the anti-slavery Republican Party to stand for president. Most Republicans did not favour outlawing slavery, but the party opposed the extension of slavery in the West. Facing a divided opposition Democratic Party, Lincoln won a narrow victory.

As president

Throughout his presidency, Lincoln led a nation at war with itself. At first he fought to restore the Union as it was, but on 1 January 1863 he issued a proclamation, freeing all the slaves in the Confederacy. To achieve this, against his wishes, he had to defeat the south.

Confederate flag   Union flag

Leaving the Union

In December 1860, a month after Lincoln won the presidential election, the slave state of South Carolina voted to leave the Union. By the following June, 10 more states had left and formed the Confederacy. Five slave-owning states decided to remain in the Union.

Assassination

On 14 April 1865, Lincoln and his wife visited Ford's Theatre in Washington to see a performance of *Our American Cousin*. John Wilkes Booth, a 26-year-old pro-Confederate actor, shot and killed the president. Lincoln lay in state at the White House for two weeks before being buried in Illinois.

Lincoln regretted the loss of life on both sides.

The Civil War

Civil war broke out in April 1861 when Confederate troops shelled the Union-held Fort Sumter in Charleston Harbor, South Carolina. War raged for four years, until Confederate forces, led by Robert E. Lee, surrendered to General Ulysses S. Grant at Appomattox court house, Virginia.

Lincoln's administration

Lincoln presided over an administration divided between radicals who demanded the end of slavery and conservatives who feared the Union would lose the war. Lincoln, however, managed to hold his government together.

ABRAHAM LINCOLN

1809	Born in rural Kentucky
1834	Elected to state legislature
1836	Qualifies as a lawyer
1842	Marries Mary Todd
1847	Elected to US Congress
1859	Runs unsuccessfully for US senate against Stephen Douglas
1860	Elected president of the USA
1861	Civil war breaks out
1863	Issues Emancipation Proclamation
1863	Makes address at Gettysburg, Pennsylvania
1865	Assassinated in Washington D.C.

FIND OUT MORE

AMERICAN CIVIL WAR   SLAVERY   TRUTH, SOJOURNER   UNITED STATES, HISTORY OF

NORTHERN IRELAND

PART OF THE UNITED KINGDOM, Northern Ireland occupies the northeastern corner of Ireland. It is a green country with a mild climate; much of the land is used for farming. Queen Elizabeth is the head of state, and until recently Northern Ireland was governed from London. The province has had a troubled history, with its population divided by religious and cultural issues. However, the terrorist violence of the 1970s and 1980s has been replaced by a new peace initiative, promising a brighter future.

The region
Northern Ireland is bordered by the Republic of Ireland to the south and west. The province remained in the United Kingdom when Ireland became independent in 1920. Its six counties were part of Ulster, one of Ireland's four traditional kingdoms.

Landscape

Most of Northern Ireland is flat, fertile pastureland. Near the coast there are some low mountains, including the famous Mountains of Mourne in the southeast. The many loughs (lakes) contain a variety of fish, including salmon, trout, and pike; many kinds of wildlife inhabit the marshy shores.

Farming
About 30 per cent of the population live in rural areas, the highest proportion of country dwellers in the United Kingdom. Farms provide a livelihood for most of the rural population – they tend to raise both livestock and crops. Pigs and chickens are main agricultural exports, as are milk and potatoes.

A typical Irish country scene

Giant's Causeway
Off the coast of County Antrim lies the Giant's Causeway, a surreal "path" of 37,000 basalt columns. Legend has it that the hero Finn MacCool built the causeway so that he could walk across the sea to Scotland. In fact, it formed after a massive underground explosion, 60 million years ago. As volcanic rock spewed into the sea, it cooled and solidified into columns.

Lough Neagh is a popular site for fishing.

Loughs of Northern Ireland
Many loughs dot the countryside, including Lough Neagh, the largest lake in the United Kingdom. The two lakes of Lough Erne fill a third of County Fermanagh. The lower lough has many small islands, some still bearing the ruins of ancient Christian settlements.

Tourism

The tourist industry in Northern Ireland was badly hit by the Troubles in the past. However, in recent years holidaymakers have begun visiting the region. The Giant's Causeway has been a major attraction since the 17th century. In addition, there are sandy beaches in the southeast, beautiful countryside, and excellent fishing.

Irish castle

Belfast

Belfast, on the northeast coast, is the region's prosperous capital city. It has modernized dockyards and is one of the United Kingdom's major ports. Shipbuilding was once its most important industry, but has declined. Now other types of manufacturing help to maintain the city as the industrial centre of Northern Ireland.

Belfast city centre

The Troubles

Since Ireland was partitioned in 1920, there has often been division and violence in the North between Unionists and Republicans. In 1968, Catholic civil rights marches were the catalyst for a sustained period of sectarian violence known as the Troubles, which lasted until 1997. Terrorism by minority groups on both sides led to more than 3,400 deaths.

Protestant marches are a frequent source of conflict.

Republicans
Republicans are mostly Catholic. They wish to break ties with the United Kingdom and unite the North with the Republic of Ireland. The Irish Republican Army (IRA) is a terrorist organization that has used bombing and murder to pursue this end. The IRA's political wing is called Sinn Fein.

Unionists
Unionists are Protestants who want Northern Ireland to stay in the United Kingdom – although they favour self-government for the province. They too have terrorist organisations, such as the Ulster Volunteer Force, as well as political parties.

Republican murals call for withdrawal of British troops.

Peace process
In 1997, both sides agreed to a cease-fire. Multi-party peace talks, involving both British and Irish governments, led to the "Good Friday Agreement" of April 1998. This created a self-governing assembly for Northern Ireland, where all the province's people will be represented. As part of the agreement, the Republic gets a limited say in some matters of Northern Ireland policy.

FIND OUT MORE   CASTLES   FARMING   IRELAND, HISTORY OF   UNITED KINGDOM, HISTORY OF

OLYMPICS, SYDNEY

ON 12 MAY 2000, the Olympic flame will be lit at Olympia, Greece, the site of the ancient Olympic Games. A torch will carry the flame by relay to Australia, and from 15 September to 1 October, the flame will burn at the Sydney Olympic stadium during the greatest sporting festival in the world. The budget for the Sydney Olympics, and the Paralympic Games that follow them, is a staggering $2.6 billion Australian.

Bondi Beach

Other venues
Some sports will be contested away from Olympic Park. Sailing will take place at Sydney Harbour, while beach volleyball will be contested at Bondi Beach. Sydney's West and Darling Harbours are the sites of other Olympic competitions.

Sydney Olympic Park

Situated west of the city centre, Sydney Olympic Park occupies 760 hectares at Homebush Bay. The park contains many new sports centres and the solar-powered Olympic village. Most of the sports events will take place in the Park. The new Olympic Stadium is to host the opening and closing ceremonies.

Security
The Games provide an opportunity to draw worldwide attention to grievances, so security is a major concern. Some past protests have ended in tragedy. In 1972, 15 people were killed at the Munich Olympics, after Palestinian terrorists held some of the Israeli team hostage.

Millennium games
More than 10,000 athletes from 200 countries – accompanied by 5,100 support staff – will compete in the first Olympic Games of the new millennium. The Games will be covered by about 15,000 media representatives, and will have a worldwide audience of more than 3.5 billion people.

Olympic village
For the first time ever, all of the athletes will live in one village. Each sports venue is less than 35 minutes' travel away, so many athletes will be able to walk to their events. After the Olympic Games, the village will be altered to provide facilities for the 7,000 athletes and officials of the Paralympic Games. When these Games are over, the village will become part of a new Sydney suburb.

Sydney Showground and Baseball Stadium
Sydney International Aquatic Centre
Hockey Centre
Athletic Centre
Olympic Stadium
Sydney SuperDome
Main Press Centre

Sports centres in the Olympic Park

New sporting events

The 28 medal sports at the Sydney Olympic Games will cover almost 300 individual and team events. Taekwondo and the triathlon will become medal sports for the first time. There will also be new disciplines, such as trampolining, but no demonstration sports will be featured.

Competitors wear protective headgear

Taekwondo
This combat sport originated in Korea before AD1000. Its name means "the way of the hand and foot". Each contestant wears a body guard marked with red or blue areas, and scores points by striking an oppponent in these coloured areas. A competitor may kick, but not punch, an opponent's head.

Women's events
Women could not compete in the first modern Olympic Games in 1896. Since then, more women's events have gradually been added to the Olympic programme. At the Sydney Olympics, most sports will have events for both men and women. New women's events include pole-vaulting, water polo, weightlifting, and hammer-throwing.

Taekwondo combatants

Environment
The Sydney Games were planned with the aim of protecting the environment. The Olympic Park was developed around existing ecosystems. A railway station and a ferry terminal have been built to encourage people to use public transport. Rainwater collected from the stadium's roof irrigates its pitch. Design features keep the stadium cool and minimize the need for air-conditioning.

White-faced Egret

FIND OUT MORE — ATHLETICS — AUSTRALIA — AUSTRALIAN ENVIRONMENT — COMBAT SPORTS — GYMNASTICS

RED CROSS

THIS HUMANITARIAN ORGANIZATION was set up in the 19th century to help the wounded on the battlefield, regardless of their political or religious beliefs. Today, the International Red Cross and Red Crescent Movement attempts to prevent and ease human suffering wherever it is found, and to promote respect for human life.

Volunteers are trained in first aid.

Services

The Red Cross movement exists to ease suffering and protect life and health. National societies work towards this aim in both war and peace. During times of war or natural disaster, the society provides emergency relief, while in peacetime volunteers promote health and welfare in their local communities.

War and disasters

Red Cross volunteers care for wounded soldiers and civilians and tend the victims of natural disasters, such as earthquakes or hurricanes. The society organizes relief programmes, helps destroyed communities to rebuild their lives, aids refugees and asylum seekers, and reunites separated families. It also provides a message service if normal communications break down.

Organization

The Red Cross was founded in 1863, in Geneva, Switzerland. Before 1863, there was no legal solution to the humanitarian problems that arose because of war, such as the protection of medical staff caring for wounded soldiers. The International Committee of the Red Cross (ICRC) provided a single body that would deal with these issues in law.

Jean Henri Dunant

A Swiss businessman, Dunant (1828–1910) founded the Red Cross. Appalled by the suffering of the wounded soldiers in the Austro-Sardinian War (1859), he organized voluntary medical aid. In the book *A Memory of Solferino* (1862), Dunant proposed that every nation should form voluntary relief services.

Red Cross parcels help victims of war.

Geneva Conventions

The Geneva Convention of 1864 established international agreement on the treatment of people in wartime. Delegates from 12 European nations agreed a code of conduct, which established the neutral role of the Red Cross to allow it to protect and tend to victims of war. There were four further Conventions – two in 1907, 1929, and 1949. They deal with the protection of those wounded or shipwrecked at sea, prisoners-of-war, and civilians during wartime.

Peacetime

In peacetime, Red Cross societies work to benefit their local communities. Tasks include collecting blood for transfusions, running first aid and safety courses, supplementing local health services with nursing and health programmes, and caring for the sick and disabled. The local organizations also train junior volunteers, and run "disaster preparedness" courses.

Children attend a Red Cross nursery school.

Around the world

The work of national Red Cross societies differs according to the needs and culture of the region. However, each society upholds the principles of the movement, which include neutrality, impartiality, and independence. While they must work within the laws of their country, societies cannot side with that country in a dispute. In some countries, Red Cross volunteers operate in dangerous conditions.

Emergency relief

When the International Committee of the Red Cross requests emergency relief for a war-torn region, local organizations respond by sending delegates and occasionally supplies or medicine. In Africa, for example, this relief has been used to help victims of civil and guerrilla warfare, but problems have included the murder of volunteers.

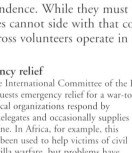

The red crescent is the official emblem for Muslim countries.

Governing bodies

The International Committee of the Red Cross (ICRC) comprises a council of 25 Swiss citizens. It acts as an intermediary during wartime and seeks to improve the Geneva Conventions. The International Federation of Red Cross and Red Crescent Societies encourages the development of new national societies and co-ordinates relief efforts outside war zones.

Red Crescent

The original symbol of the Red Cross was a red cross on a white background. It had no religious significance, but was a visible sign to the wounded, representing protection and medical aid. Since 1986, the name of the organisation has included the Red Crescent, which was first adopted during the Russo-Turkish war of 1876–78.

Clara Barton

Originally a teacher, Clara Barton (1821–1912) worked as a nurse during the American Civil War, then with the International Red Cross during the Franco-Prussian War. In 1881 she established the first branch of the Red Cross in the USA.

FIND OUT MORE   FIRST AID   FLAGS   MEDICINE   PEACE MOVEMENTS   SWITZERLAND AND AUSTRIA   UNITED NATIONS   WARFARE

SCOTLAND

SCOTLAND OCCUPIES THE NORTHERN third of Britain, as well as the hundreds of islands scattered around its coast. This beautiful land encompasses rugged mountains and deep, still lochs (lakes) in the north, and rolling pasture-land in its centre. Old Scottish customs are best preserved in the highland villages, but Scots everywhere treasure their cultural heritage. In 1999 the Scottish people elected members for a Scottish parliament.

The region
The Scottish mainland is usually seen as three main regions: the mountainous Highlands, populated by rural communities; the Central Lowlands, where most people live; and the Southern Uplands, situated on the borders with England. The Western Isles and Shetland Islands lie off Scotland's north coast.

Scottish National Party
This political party was formed in 1928, and first won a seat in parliament during a by-election in 1945. The SNP sees devolution as a first step towards their ultimate aim of independence for Scotland.

Scottish devolution
After a series of conflicts, Scotland and England were joined under one crown in 1707 by the Act of Union. Scotland was governed from London, but maintained separate judicial, educational, and legal systems. However, recent political developments led to a referendum on devolution in 1997, in which 80 per cent of voters voted "Yes" to self-government.

Nationalists campaign for independence

Scottish parliament
The new Scottish parliament sat for the first time in 1999 – the first such assembly for 300 years. Led by a First Minister, the parliament has the power to set policy on issues of health and education in Scotland, as well as vary the rate of income tax. The parliament sits in Edinburgh; a new parliament building opens in 2000.

Edinburgh festival
Every summer, the Scottish capital Edinburgh hosts one of the most important arts festivals in the world. For three weeks, arts-lovers feast on opera, ballet, music, and drama, brought to them by performers from many different countries. The festival began in 1947.

Culture
The Scots maintain many unique and recognizable traditions. While most people speak English, about 80,000 people are Gaelic speakers (mainly in the Highlands and Islands). Sport is a popular pastime; the national game, golf, originated in 15th-century Scotland. The arts also thrive, especially in the two main cities of Glasgow and Edinburgh.

Highland games
Highland games are held throughout the Scottish Highlands from spring to autumn. Kilt-wearing competitors gather to toss the caber (a large tree trunk), throw the hammer and the shot put, dance, and play the bagpipes.

Chair designed by Rennie Mackintosh

Cultural Glasgow
As a former centre of industry, Glasgow was once called the "Second City of the Empire" (after London). Today it is Scotland's main home for the arts, and contains many notable art galleries, museums, and buildings, such as the Glasgow School of Art, designed by Charles Rennie Mackintosh (1868–1928).

Industry
Before the coal pit closures of the 1980s, many Scottish people worked in heavy industry. Today, most work in the service and manufacturing industries. Chemicals, electronic equipment, industrial machinery, woollen textiles, and malt whisky are the main manufactured goods, while revenues from tourism are on the increase. Most factories in Scotland are clustered in the central lowlands, where 75 per cent of the population lives.

Oil
Large fields of natural gas and petrol lie off the northeast coast of Scotland. North Sea oil was first brought ashore in the 1970s. Since then it has become Scotland's main export, supplying most energy needs for the UK, and also being sold to other European countries.

Farming
Some of the best farmland in Britain is found on the Scottish Lowlands. The farming regions are very hilly, so most farmers keep livestock rather than grow crops. Scottish livestock is often bred to cope with winter weather. Only 15 per cent of all Scottish people depend on farming for a living, even though much of the country is turned over to agriculture.

Clans and tartans
From the 12th century, Highland society was divided into clans – tribes ruled by all-powerful chiefs. Each clan had its own distinctive tartan.

The Campbells of Western Scotland were feared for their military prowess. They fought the Jacobites in 1746 at the Battle of Culloden.

The Stuarts ruled Scotland from 1371 to 1603. Their famous motto was: "no one harms me with impunity".

The MacLeods of the Western Isles originally came from Scandinavia, but their chief made his home in Dunvegan Castle, Isle of Skye.

FIND OUT MORE   FARMING   FESTIVALS   OIL   UNITED KINGDOM   UNITED KINGDOM, HISTORY OF

TUDORS

ONE OF THE MOST FAMOUS of all English ruling families were the Tudors, who reigned from 1485 to 1603. The Tudors ended the civil war between the noble houses of York and Lancaster. They improved the economy, made England more prosperous, and presided over great artistic achievements. A series of disputes over religion led to the formation of the Church of England. Many people lost their lives during the resulting turbulence, which made the Tudor era a time of conflict and unhappiness.

Fur-trimmed gown

Broad, "duck-bill" shoes, with slashing

Henry VII

The Lancastrian Henry Tudor (r.1485–1509) defeated the House of York at the Battle of Bosworth Field. He became King Henry VII and married a Yorkist princess to unite the two families. Henry kept a tight reign on power, paid off the royal debts, and developed a strict system of justice. He had to repel several claimants to the throne, including Perkin Warbeck, whom he had executed.

Henry VIII

The ambitious Henry VIII (r.1509–47) wanted England to have greater international power and political independence. He was also desperate for a male heir who would be a strong successor. When his first wife, Catherine of Aragon, bore him only a daughter, Henry divorced her. To do this, Henry broke with the Roman Catholic Church and established the Church of England. Henry's six wives had tragic fates. Two were executed, two were divorced, and one died. Only Catherine Parr survived him.

Edward VI

Edward (r.1547–53) was nine years old and in poor health when he became king. His uncle, the Duke of Somerset, ruled on his behalf as a "Protector". Edward introduced the English prayer-book and banned Catholicism. These actions coincided with widespread poverty during his reign, and caused discontent.

Mary I

Mary (r.1553–58), the daughter of Catherine of Aragon, came to the throne following the nine-day reign of Jane Grey. A fervent Catholic, Mary brought the old religion back to England. She had many Protestants put to death and banned the English prayer-book. Mary's marriage created an alliance with a Catholic state.

Elizabeth I

Elizabeth (r.1558–1603) ended the persecution of Protestants, brought stability back to England, and promoted trade, exploration, and the arts. Elizabeth refused to marry, as a husband would weaken her power. She survived plots to depose her and attacks from the Spanish.

Arts and culture

Under the Tudors, the arts flourished in England as never before. The royal family and the aristocracy provided enthusiastic patronage to artists. Literature enjoyed a golden age. Painters such as Nicholas Hilliard produced portraits with a new skill and realism. English music was among the finest in Europe, and ranged from witty love songs to solemn religious works.

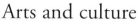

Architecture

The Tudor period saw a boom in house-building. Smaller homes were rebuilt with materials available locally, such as timber, stone, and brick. The large houses of Elizabethan nobility looked striking from the outside. They had long galleries and featured big rooms decorated with ornate plasterwork and wooden panelling.

Hampton Court

Literature

Elizabethan England produced some of the greatest poets and playwrights of all time. Dramatists such as William Shakespeare and Christopher Marlowe wrote tragedies, comedies, and plays about English history that are still performed today. The poets Edmund Spenser, Sir Thomas Wyatt, and Sir Philip Sidney transformed English poetry. Their love poems were especially admired. They introduced new ideas and verse forms from the continent, such as the sonnet.

Philip Sidney's prose romance, *Arcadia*

Reformation

By Tudor times, many English people had become discontented with the Catholic Church. Clergymen were thought to be corrupt, and European ideas about religious reform were gaining popularity. In 1533 the Pope excommunicated Henry VIII when he divorced Catherine of Aragon. The following year, Henry established the independent Church of England.

Martin Luther

Protestantism
European reformers, such as Martin Luther, preached against a corrupt Catholic priesthood. They argued that faith should be based solely on the Bible's words, and that the Bible should be translated from Latin into the modern European languages. The Church of England did not adopt all of the Protestant ideas, but it began to use Bibles and prayer-books written in English.

Dissolution of the monasteries
Henry VIII ordered Thomas Cromwell, his Chancellor, to report on the condition and wealth of England's monasteries. Cromwell found them to be corrupt, so Henry decided to abolish them. The smaller monasteries were closed in 1536 and the larger establishments followed suit in 1539. Henry's extravagant court had left him short of money. He confiscated the lands of the monasteries and sold off their valuable possessions.

Founded in the 1120s, this priory was destroyed during the Reformation.

The gatehouse of Kirkham Priory

Thomas Cranmer

Key figures
Sir Thomas More was Henry VIII's first chancellor. He was beheaded when he refused to accept the king as head of the Church. Thomas Cromwell replaced More and presided over the reorganization of the Church, but was executed for treason. Archbishop Thomas Cranmer oversaw the creation of the English Bible and the *Book of Common Prayer*.

Daily life

Most people in Tudor England lived in the countryside and worked on the land. Their houses were made of a wooden framework filled with wattle and daub (interlaced twigs plastered with clay), and were small and cramped. Towns and cities grew to form the basis of a flourishing trading network. British merchants became wealthy through the export of iron, salt, and coal, but the export of cloth produced the greatest income.

Ruff stiffened with starch

Padded doublet

Velvet shoes decorated with embroidery

Clothes
Rich Tudors wore outfits of linen, silk, and fine wool, and stiff collars called ruffs. Women wore several layers of clothing. The bodice and skirt were visible beneath an outer gown. Male costume was elaborate. Padded doublets and sleeves were slashed to show the material underneath. Poor people had simpler costumes of coarse wool. Women wore plain gowns protected by an apron. Men wore simple doublets, breeches (short trousers), and stout leather boots or shoes.

Chessboard

Games
People worked long hours, but religious festivals and saints' days provided them with leisure time. Dice and cards were common indoor games. Board games, such as draughts, backgammon, and chess, were also played. Hunting was popular in the country, while city people amused themselves with activities such as bear-baiting, or by going to the theatre.

Tudor carpenters made furniture that was basic but durable.

Work
Country people were mixed farmers. They grew wheat for flour and raised animals for meat. There were also many sheep farmers, who sold wool to the merchants. The traditional crafts – pottery, carpentry, blacksmithery, and weaving – thrived in both the town and the country. Many people worked as servants for the wealthy merchant and noble families. Servant wages were low but they were housed and fed by their employers.

Timeline

1485 Henry VII becomes king, following the defeat of Richard III.

1487 Henry VII uses the Court of Star Chamber to provide speedy justice in criminal cases.

1509 Henry VIII becomes king.

1527 Henry VIII asks the Pope to end his marriage to Catherine of Aragon.

1536 Dissolution of the monasteries begins.

1536 The Act of Union unites Wales and England.

1543 The Act of Supremacy makes Henry VIII the head of the Church of England.

1547 Edward VI becomes king.

The death of Cranmer

1549 The first prayer-book written in English is issued.

1553 Lady Jane Grey becomes queen, but she is replaced by Mary after a nine-day reign.

1555 Protestant clergy are burned at the stake.

1558 Elizabeth I becomes queen.

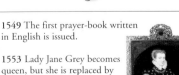
Mary, Queen of Scots

1587 Mary, Queen of Scots is executed.

1588 The English navy defeats the Spanish Armada.

1592 Thousands of Londoners are killed by an outbreak of the plague.

1603 The Tudor period ends with the death of Elizabeth I. James I becomes king of England.

FIND OUT MORE CHRISTIANITY ELIZABETH I REFORMATION SHAKESPEARE, WILLIAM UNITED KINGDOM UNITED KINGDOM, HISTORY OF

TUTU, DESMOND

ONE OF SOUTH AFRICA'S most important black leaders, Desmond Mbilo Tutu was at the forefront of the long fight against apartheid. He started a career as a a schoolteacher, became a priest, but continued teaching until he was appointed to St. Mary's Cathedral, Johannesburg. He rose rapidly to become Archbishop of Cape Town and head of the Anglican Church in South Africa.

Early life
Desmond Tutu was the son of Zachariah, a strict man who taught in mission schools. His mother, Aletta, was a gentle person who had a great influence on her son. After school Tutu went to Bantu Normal College to study for a teaching career. There he met his wife, Normalizo Leah Shenxane.

The Tutus' wedding

The priesthood

In 1958 Desmond Tutu realised that his true vocation was with the Church. He was ordained a priest in 1961, and went to London to study theology at King's College. Between 1970 and1972 he taught at the University of Botswana in Lesotho, then returned to England to become an assistant director for the World Council of Churches.

First black bishop
Between 1976 and 1978 Tutu was Bishop of Lesotho. Again, he was the first black priest to reach this rank in the Anglican Church. However, he became aware that black opposition to apartheid was mounting, and an uprising was becoming inevitable. He wrote to South Africa's prime minister, Balthazar J. Vorster, to warn him of the dangers. A few days later, violence erupted, and more than 100 people died.

Return to South Africa
Tutu returned to South Africa in 1975 to become Dean of St. Mary's Cathedral, Johannesburg. He was the first black person to hold such a high post in the Church in South Africa. At the time there was little opposition to apartheid, and most black leaders were either in exile or in prison. Tutu felt the position of his fellow blacks keenly.

Political career

Recognising the huge divide between the peoples of South Africa, Tutu became a spokesman for the oppressed black majority. Between 1978 and 1985 he served as general secretary for the South African Council of Churches, a position in which he could exert great influence. He spoke at rallies and called on other countries to impose sanctions on South Africa in support of the anti-apartheid movement.

Nobel Peace Prize

Bishop Tutu led the opposition to a new South African constitution that supported apartheid. When the constitution was voted in, violence erupted. As the government suppressed the uprising, news came that Tutu had been awarded the 1984 Nobel Peace Prize for using peaceful means of protest against apartheid. In November that year the Church appointed Tutu as Bishop of Johannesburg.

The archbishop
In September 1986 Desmond Tutu was enthroned as Archbishop of Cape Town, the highest position in the South African Anglican Church. In 1994 Tutu saw the end of his struggle, when South Africa became a democratic state.

Civil disobedience
Bishop Tutu was opposed to violence. He called on people to use civil disobedience to conduct their fight against apartheid. This did not save him from being arrested, along with other bishops, for taking part in a protest march.

Retirement

Tutu resigned as Archbishop of Cape Town in 1996. He planned to retire with his family to the United States, where he had been offered a teaching post at Emory University in Atlanta, Georgia – a coeducational establishment linked to the Methodist Church. However, Tutu agreed to postpone his retirement to chair the Truth and Reconciliation Commission.

Truth and Reconciliation Commission
Archbishop Tutu led the Truth and Reconciliation Commission from 1996 to 1998, despite being diagnosed with prostate cancer in January 1997. The commission investigated 21,000 human rights violations, considered reparations for victims, and in some cases granted amnesties for those who had confessed. Its report ran to 3,500 pages. "Accept it as an indispensable way to heal", Tutu said.

DESMOND TUTU

1931	Born at Klerksdorp, NW Region
1955	Marries Leah Shenxane
1961	Ordained a priest
1975	Made Dean of Johannesburg
1976	Appointed Bishop of Lesotho
1984	Awarded Nobel Peace Prize
1985	Becomes Bishop of Johannesburg
1986	Becomes Archbishop of Cape Town
1996	Retires as Archbishop
1996–98	Chairs Truth and Reconciliation Commission

FIND OUT MORE   GOVERNMENTS AND POLITICS   HUMAN RIGHTS   MANDELA, NELSON   SOUTH AFRICA, HISTORY OF

US CIVIL RIGHTS

ALL PEOPLE TODAY BELIEVE THAT they have a basic right to equal treatment, regardless of colour, gender, belief, or ethnic origin. These human rights become civil rights when enshrined in law. The US Constitution defines the civil rights of large sections of the population, such as Native Americans and African-Americans, women, and the disabled. Often these rights are the result of years of protest and struggle.

Civil rights and the government

The US Constitution, introduced in 1789, is the supreme law of the land. It defines how the United States is governed and sets out the rights of American citizens. State and federal courts have interpreted the Constitution in different ways, particularly over matters of civil rights. The Supreme Court can be called on to make a final judgement.

Constitution
The US Constitution consists of a preamble, seven articles, and 27 amendments. The first 10 amendments (the Bill of Rights, adopted in 1791) guarantee individual liberties, such as freedom of speech and worship. Later amendments include the 13th (1865), abolishing slavery, and the 19th (1920), recognizing women's right to vote.

Civil Rights Act of 1964
The Civil Rights Act was a landmark in the history of US civil rights. It was introduced after years of campaigning, and was designed to end discrimination based on race, colour, religion, or ethnic origin. Together with the Voting Rights Act (1965), it prohibits segregation and discrimination in public places, employment, schooling, and voting. The highly controversial act was passed by Senate after one of the longest debates in its history.

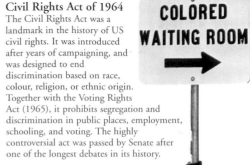

Affirmative action
Laws alone do not stop discrimination. In 1964, the US government introduced affirmative action – a system that gave women and ethnic minorities preference when applying for certain jobs and federal-funded opportunities. Some people criticised affirmative action as a form of reverse discrimination, and in 1989 the Supreme Court restricted its use.

Students from different ethnic and racial backgrounds mix freely at a modern college.

Human rights

Although many civil rights are guaranteed in the US Constitution, this in itself does not guarantee that these rights will be enforced. Oppressed minorities often form organizations and take group action to demand a change, and there are now many popular movements campaigning for better treatment of minority social groups. Organizations such as these have successfully lobbied for laws to ensure that the constitutional ideals of equality are turned into practical reality.

The work of groups like the ACLU has brought equality to the workplace.

American Civil Liberties Union (ACLU)
In 1920 Roger Baldwin (1884–1981), Jane Addams (1860–1935), and others founded the American Civil Liberties Union (ACLU) to protect the basic rights set out in the Constitution. Thousands of volunteers work for the ACLU, including lawyers who work for free – since its beginning, it has supported nearly every major civil rights court case.

Equal Rights Amendment (ERA)
In 1923 shortly after American women won the vote, Congress adopted the Equal Rights Amendment Act, outlawing discrimination on the grounds of sex. In 1972 moves to make this the 27th amendment to the Constitution failed because of opposition from some political and religious groups.

Women's rights

American women began campaigning for voting rights in the 19th century. Early activists set up the first Women's Rights Convention at Seneca Falls, New York, in 1848. The right to vote was won in 1920 and job discrimination was banned in 1964. Since then, women have continued to campaign for greater equality and opportunities at work and in other areas.

Girls today need not worry about conforming to stereotypes.

National Organization of Women (NOW)
NOW is the largest and most broadly based women's rights group in the USA. It was set up in 1966 by a group of feminists, including Betty Friedan (b. 1921). NOW has campaigned actively for equal rights, equal pay, child care, birth control, and paid maternity leave.

African-American rights

From the 1870s, the southern states of the United States actively prevented African-Americans from enjoying the same rights as other Americans. A "separate but equal" policy operated in the South for many years, and kept white and black Americans apart. However, African-Americans fought back, particularly from the 1950s onwards, when the full-blown civil rights movement emerged, headed by Martin Luther King Jr.

Jesse Jackson

Born in Greenville, South Carolina, Jesse Jackson (b. 1941) is a politician, civil rights activist, and Baptist minister. He was closely involved with Martin Luther King Jr. and the civil rights movement of the 1960s. In 1971 he founded Operation PUSH (People United to Save Humanity), a Chicago-based organization advocating African-American self-help. In 1984 and 1988 he became the first African-American to make a serious bid for the presidency.

National Association for the Advancement of Colored Peoples (NAACP)

One of the earliest organizations to campaign for racial equality was the NAACP. It was created in 1910 by William E.B. Du Bois (1868–1963) and a group of concerned white Americans. Its first aim was the abolition of lynching in the southern states, which it achieved in the 1950s. It also worked towards the desegregation of schools, which was achieved in 1954.

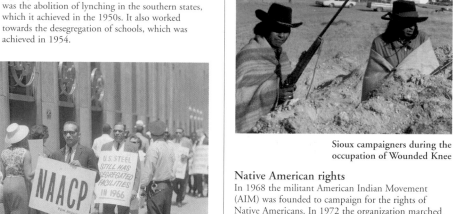

Sioux campaigners during the occupation of Wounded Knee

Native American rights

In 1968 the militant American Indian Movement (AIM) was founded to campaign for the rights of Native Americans. In 1972 the organization marched on Washington D.C., and briefly occupied the Bureau of Indian Affairs. A year later, AIM led 200 Sioux in a takeover of the historic site at Wounded Knee, South Dakota, to draw attention to government policy towards Native Americans. In 1988 the government finally granted Native Americans improved rights over their lands, but AIM continues to campaign for full native sovereignty and self-government, in line with treaties the US government agreed in the 19th century.

Gay activism

The modern US gay rights movement emerged after the Stonewall riot of 1969. A number of groups formed to fight anti-homosexuality laws and to overturn anti-gay discrimination in housing and work. By the early 1990s, most states had removed their anti-gay laws, although active discrimination and attacks on gay men continue. Most recently, gay activists have focused on challenging anti-gay discrimination in the armed forces.

Pink triangle has become an emblem of the gay pride movement.

Symbols of gay and lesbian protest

Gay pride

For centuries, gays and lesbians concealed their sexuality and were forced underground. A large element of the battle for gay rights has been the struggle for the right to "come out" and be accepted by society. Gay pride marches and campaigns aim to reinforce confidence among gays themselves, as well as encouraging wider understanding.

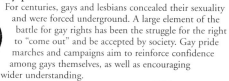

Stonewall riots

On 28 June 1969, New York police raided the Stonewall Inn, a gay bar in the city. Raids like this were common at the time, but on this occasion, people in the bar actively resisted – the first time such action had been taken in the United States. A 45-minute riot developed, and 13 people were arrested. This simply worsened the situation, and rioting continued on the following nights. The gay rights movement commemorates Stonewall every year.

AIDS activism

In the 1980s, gay rights activists became primarily concerned with challenging the hostility and discrimination that accompanied the arrival of AIDS (Acquired Immune Deficiency Syndrome), which initially affected mainly homosexual men. The AIDS Memorial Quilt Project was set up in 1987 to increase public awareness of the enormity of the epidemic. Each square on the quilt represents the life of a person who has died of the disease.

FIND OUT MORE

HUMAN RIGHTS   KING, MARTIN LUTHER   NATIVE AMERICANS   UNITED STATES, HISTORY OF   WOMEN'S MOVEMENT

US NATIONAL PARKS

THE NATIONAL PARK SYSTEM of the USA consists of more than 350 sites, which cover a combined area of more than 80 million acres of land. These protected areas were established to conserve the natural, historical, and cultural inheritance of the USA. Their recreational uses range from backpacking and sightseeing to quiet enjoyment and spiritual refreshment. The US Park Service looks after and manages the national parks, together with other agencies.

Yellowstone

The US government declared Yellowstone a national park in 1872, making it the world's oldest such park. Its 2.2 million acres are rich in wildlife and contain the world's largest area of geysers, as well as waterfalls and canyons. Yellowstone is one of the few remaining refuges for many species, such as bison, bears, and cougars.

Types of site

The best known of the USA's protected sites are the areas managed for ecosystem preservation and recreation. These are generally known as national parks. The National Parks System also includes monuments, battlefields, seashores, historical sites, and managed resource areas.

Gorge is 1.6 km (1 mile) wide.

National parks

National parks are large areas of protected landscape with beautiful or unusual features, and with a rich diversity of wild animals and plantlife. They often include wilderness areas with little human access. Although the parks are open to visitors for recreational purposes, the use of their resources is strictly controlled. Any activities must be in keeping with conservation objectives. The national park designation allows mountain ranges, forests, swamplands, and even cave systems to be protected.

Grand Canyon, Arizona

Historical sites

The history of a country is of great value. The protected historical sites mark key events in US history. They include the birthplaces of prominent persons and former presidents, and military posts of significance.

Birthplace of President John F. Kennedy

Barrel contains spiral grooves.

Military parks and battlefields

Many fierce battles were fought during the four years of the American Civil War (1861–65). Several places that saw major turning points in this war are conserved as military parks and battlefields, such as Gettysburg National Military Park.

Gettysburg, Pennsylvania

Parks and people

The US National Park Service provides facilities that enable visitors to use protected areas for recreational and leisure purposes. The contribution that Native Americans have made to these landscapes is becoming appreciated. Agreements that enable Native Americans to resume traditional practices within national parks signify a more just approach to park management.

Redwood in Sequoia Park

Park staff

To combine site protection with sustainable tourism, Park Service staff are experts recruited from many fields. Naturalists advise on wildlife management. Landscape architects design buildings that do not harm the environment. Engineers devise environmentally friendly methods of waste disposal. Staff also encourage the stewardship of private lands outside park boundaries.

History of the Park Service

Yellowstone National Park was the inspiration for the establishment of other national parks. Many new sites soon followed, such as Sequoia National Park. The US National Park Service was set up in 1916. It promotes sustainable tourism and publishes guidelines on caring for these valuable sites.

Visitors

More than 250 million people visit the national parks every year. The overuse of popular areas can cause site degradation, so visitor access to sites is graded. Core areas provide a few basic amenities, while recreational sites have lodges and campsites.

FIRE DANGER
LOW
TODAY!
PREVENT FOREST FIRES

FIND OUT MORE CAMPING AND HIKING CONSERVATION MOUNTAIN WILDLIFE NATIVE AMERICANS NORTH AMERICA NORTH AMERICAN WILDLIFE UNITED STATES, HISTORY OF

US PRESIDENTS

THE PRESIDENT OF THE United States of America is probably the most powerful person in the world. According to the US Constitution, he or she must be US-born and over 35 years old. So far, all presidents have been men. The president's main duty is to protect the Constitution and enforce laws made by Congress, but other areas of responsibility range from the legal system to foreign policy.

History of the office

When the US Constitution was written in 1789, the idea of an elected president was a new one, so many balances to the president's power were incorporated, including a strong Congress. The most successful presidents were often the strongest, such as Washington and Lincoln. Twentieth-century presidents used their power for many different ends: Wilson reformed the economy, Franklin D. Roosevelt pulled the USA out of the Great Depression, and Truman steered it through the Cold War.

The job

The most important task of the president is to form policies and recommend new laws to Congress. A president has power of veto to stop any new bill becoming law – although this can be overruled by a large majority in Congress. The president appoints a cabinet to help run the federal government, while presidential advisors help to shape military and economic policy.

Election

Presidential elections take place every four years in November. People of each state vote for members of a 538-strong "Electoral College", and for the candidate of their choice. The candidate who attracts most votes in a state gains the support of all that state's Electoral College members. The winner is the candidate with a majority of the votes in the Electoral College.

Powers

The president wields a huge influence through the appointment of federal officials, who must obey Presidential orders. The president also acts as commander-in-chief of the armed forces, and in times of war may be granted even greater powers.

President in action

One of the president's most important responsibilities is to oversee the relations of the United States with other nations, negotiating treaties and other agreements with foreign powers, and deciding whether the US should recognise new nations and foreign governments. The president also appoints ambassadors and consuls, attends conferences with overseas leaders, and works with the secretary of state to manage foreign relations.

Daily life

Presidential life is very varied. At the White House, the day is divided between working in the Oval Office and hosting official functions. The president travels widely in the USA and abroad, flying on Air Force One (one of several specially-converted Boeing 747s). There may also be time to relax at Camp David, the presidential retreat in Maryland, some 110 km (68 miles) from the White House.

Cabinet rooms

The first lady

The president's wife is known as the "first lady". During the 20th century, this mainly social role has moved to a closer involvement in matters of state. Eleanor Roosevelt greatly expanded her role through campaigns for child welfare, slum-clearance, and equal rights. Hillary Clinton, with her interest in social policy, continues this tradition.

Eleanor Roosevelt

Scandals

The pressures and temptations of power have led several presidents to become involved in scandals. In the Watergate scandal, President Richard Nixon was involved in attempts to cover up his staff's illegal activities during the 1972 election campaign. Nixon was eventually forced to resign. More recently, President Bill Clinton has been accused of lying under oath about an extramarital affair.

President Kennedy moments before his assassination

First Lady Jackie Kennedy

Assassinations

Presidents are particularly vulnerable to attack by political extremists because they are powerful people who frequently appear in public. Four presidents have been murdered while in office. Abraham Lincoln and James A. Garfield were both shot by fanatical opponents. William McKinley was gunned down by an anarchist in 1901. John F. Kennedy was shot in 1963 by Lee Harvey Oswald, who was himself killed shortly afterwards.

FIND OUT MORE

AMERICAN REVOLUTION · GOVERNMENTS AND POLITICS · UNITED STATES, HISTORY OF

Presidents of the USA

1789–1797 George Washington was a revolutionary commander and the first president.

1801–1809 Thomas Jefferson drafted the Declaration of Independence.

1809–1817 James Madison played a major role in shaping the Constitution.

1825–1829 John Quincy Adams was the only son of a president to serve as president.

1841–1841 William Henry Harrison was the first president to die while in office.

1865–1869 Andrew Johnson was the first president to be impeached (tried by Congress).

1877–1881 Rutherford Birchard Hayes had the first telephone in the White House installed.

1881–1881 James Abram Garfield was assassinated only six months after he took office.

1885–1889 S. Grover Cleveland was the only president to serve two non-consecutive terms.

1897–1901 William McKinley helped the US gain its first major overseas possessions.

1901–1909 Theodore Roosevelt, at 42 years of age, was the youngest president ever sworn in.

1909–1913 William Howard Taft needed a special bathtub because he was a very large man.

1913–1921 Woodrow Wilson attempted to bring the United States into the League of Nations.

1933–1945 Franklin Delano Roosevelt was the only president to be elected four times.

1945–1953 Harry S. Truman ordered the dropping of atomic bombs during World War II.

1953–1961 Dwight David Eisenhower was a war hero who wanted to achieve world peace.

1961–1963 John F. Kennedy was the first Roman Catholic to be elected president.

1969–1974 Richard Nixon resigned when he faced impeachment over the Watergate scandal.

1993– William Jefferson Clinton was the first president to stand trial for lying while under oath, but remained extremely popular.

1974–1977 Gerald Ford was the only president not to be elected either president or vice-president.

1981–1989 Ronald Reagan was the first Hollywood actor to become president.

1989–1993 George Bush saw the end of the Cold War and led during the Persian Gulf War.

VICTORIANS

QUEEN VICTORIA RULED Britain from 1837 until 1901 – the longest reign by a British monarch. Historians call her reign the "Victorian Age", and describe the British people of that time as Victorians. During Victoria's reign technology and industry developed rapidly, making Britain the world's first and leading industrial nation. The effects transformed every aspect of British society, from schooling and politics to the home and work. Outside Britain, Victoria ruled over the largest empire the world had ever seen.

The British Royal Family and some European relations in 1897.

Queen Victoria

Family life

Victoria married her German cousin, Albert, whom she adored. He advised her on political matters and was a caring father. They had nine children, and their close family life provided a model for the nation. Through her children's marriages Victoria became linked to all the major European royal houses. When Prince Albert died in 1861, Victoria went into deep mourning.

Queen Victoria

Victoria was only 18 when she came to the throne. As a constitutional monarch, she was not allowed to decide affairs of state – only Parliament had those powers. However, she was a forceful and determined monarch, who took an active interest in Britain's government, working closely with her prime ministers, such as Melbourne and Disraeli.

Queen Victoria in 1842

Railways

From 1840, the growth of industry triggered a rapid boom in the building of railways. In 1843, there were 3,123 km (1,952 miles) of railways – by 1855 this figure had risen to 12,800 km (8,000 miles). By the late 1800s, railways were also carrying increasing numbers of passengers.

The Forth rail bridge, Scotland

Engineers and engineering

A leading figure in railway engineering was Isambard Kingdom Brunel (1805–59), who planned the lines, bridges, tunnels, and viaducts of the Great Western Railway. He also designed the *Great Western*, the first ship to cross the Atlantic using only steam power. The railways were built by navvies, using picks and shovels and working in huge gangs. The Forth Rail Bridge was the first major steel-built bridge in the world; it is one of the greatest engineering achievements of the period.

Industry

Between 1837 and 1901, Britain rapidly became industrialized. Steam-powered machinery, first introduced in the 18th century, revolutionized the way that goods were made. After 1830, manufacture increasingly moved into factories. Coal and iron output soared to meet the rising demand for goods. New techniques, such as the Bessemer steel process, stimulated steel production, and lead to new industries like engineering and shipbuilding.

The Great Exhibition

By 1850 Britain was the world's leading manufacturing nation. To celebrate the new industrial age, Prince Albert planned a great international exhibition, the first of its kind. It opened in London's Hyde Park in 1851. The centrepiece was the exhibition hall, a huge structure made of glass and cast-iron. Nicknamed the "Crystal Palace", it was a monument to Victorian engineering.

The glass ceiling was 19 m (62 ft) high.

The hall was built from identical prefabricated sections.

A cast-iron frame supported 300,000 glass panes.

The exhibition contained thousands of exhibits: arts and crafts, raw materials, machinery, and manufactured goods.

Inside the Great Exhibition hall

Paddington Station

Railway stations

Railways transformed Britain, as stations were built in towns and cities wherever trains stopped. Some stations, such as St. Pancras, London, were very ornate structures of glass and iron. Middle-class Victorians favoured this rather fussy architectural style, which was known as Gothic Revival and which symbolised the achievements of Victorian Britain.

Daily life

Industrialization created two new social classes – a wealthy middle class, which owned many of the new factories, and a large working class, consisting of the men and women who made the new industrial goods. There was a huge gap between them. The middle class enjoyed a comfortable life, but working people lived in terrible poverty for much of the 19th century.

Punch and Judy shows were performed at the seaside.

Housing

For middle-class Victorians, the ideal home provided a calm refuge from the world of work. The middle class lived in smart town houses, and later in the century they moved into suburban areas. By contrast, working-class housing was often cramped, squalid, and filthy. Sometimes many people lived in one room, often in cheap slum housing that was built in new industrial cities such as Birmingham or Manchester.

Typical working-class housing

Punch and Judy puppets – popular seaside entertainment

Leisure

Middle-class families relaxed at home by playing the piano, singing, reading, and entertaining guests. From the 1860s, life began to improve for the working class. The working day was shortened, and a law of 1871 introduced bank holidays. Working-class people flocked to the new seaside resorts, such as Blackpool and Scarborough, made more accessible, and sometimes even created, by the railways. The music hall was popular, as were team sports like football.

Work

Victorian middle-class men worked as industrialists, bankers, and professionals; it was not considered appropriate for middle-class women to work. Working-class men toiled as farm labourers, factory hands, or engineers; working-class women were employed in factories, as needleworkers, or as domestic servants. Working conditions were often dangerous.

Factory workers

Politics

Until the 19th century, only landowners could vote. By 1884 middle-class and working-class men had won the right to vote, but women were excluded. The Conservative Party emerged in the 1830s, the Liberals in the1850s, and in 1893, the Independent Labour Party was created to represent working people.

Trade Union banner

Social reform

At the start of Victoria's reign, cities were overcrowded, the working day was long, wages were low, and sickness and poverty were widespread. Parliament passed factory, education, and housing acts to improve social conditions.

Study your Health for 5/-
MACKENZIE'S CLINICAL THERMOMETER.
Healthcare improved rapidly.

Education

Wealthy Victorian boys went to private schools, while wealthy girls were educated at home. Poor children went to "ragged" (charity) schools where they learned basic reading, writing, and arithmetic, and sometimes history and geography.

Trade unions

To improve their working rights and conditions, workers formed trade unions. At first they met bitter opposition, but in the 1850s workers such as miners formed powerful unions that negotiated improvements. Trade unions were legalized in 1871.

Empire building

Under Queen Victoria, the British Empire reached its height. It was essentially a trading empire, importing raw materials such as cotton from India, and exporting goods made in British factories. The empire covered more than one-fifth of the world and contained more than 25 per cent of the world's population.

Empress of India

India was Britain's prize possession. British involvement in India was based on trading stations set up in the 1600s. After the 1857 Indian Mutiny – an army mutiny – the British government made India part of the empire. In 1876, Victoria gained the title Empress of India.

Koh-I-Noor diamond given to Victoria in 1876

Scramble for Africa

During the 1880s, many European countries, particularly Germany, France, and Britain, competed for territories in Africa, in what was known as the "scramble for Africa". The European nations sought new sources of raw materials and markets for manufactured goods. Britain gained the most territory. By 1900 it had made Kenya, Uganda, Nigeria, and southern Africa part of its empire.

Natural History Museum

Victorians explorers and missionaries travelled across the empire, making new discoveries and promoting Victorian values of thrift, enterprise, and Christian faith. In Britain libraries and museums were established. The Natural History Museum opened in 1860, financed by profits from the Great Exhibition.

Timeline

1819 Victoria is born in London.

1837 Victoria becomes queen, following the death of her uncle, William IV.

1838 The People's Charter, presented to parliament, demands parliamentary reform and votes for all.

Corn

1840 Victoria marries Prince Albert.

1846 The Corn Laws, which imposed taxes on imported corn, are removed. This marks the beginning of free trade, and opens up new markets for British goods.

1848 Potato famine in Ireland. About one million Irish people die and many thousands emigrate.

1854–56 Britain enters Crimean War to prevent Russian expansion.

1857–58 Indian Mutiny against British rule.

1861 Prince Albert dies.

1864 Factory Act prohibits children under eight from working in factories.

Victoria Cross

1870 Forster's Education Act makes primary schooling available to all.

1876 Victoria becomes Empress of India.

1887 Queen Victoria celebrates her Golden Jubilee.

1899 Boer War begins in South Africa.

1901 Queen Victoria dies.

FIND OUT MORE   AFRICA, HISTORY OF   EMPIRES   EXPLORERS   INDIA, HISTORY OF   INDUSTRIAL REVOLUTION   TRAINS AND RAILWAYS   UNITED KINGDOM, HISTORY OF

WALES

WALES OCCUPIES A WIDE WESTERN peninsula on the island of Britain. The Welsh people retain a strong national identity, although Wales has been bound to England since the 13th century and takes the British monarch as its head of state. The introduction of the Welsh Assembly in 1999 gives Wales a limited amount of home rule.

The region
Wales is a small country, taking up only 10 per cent of Britain. It is bordered by the Irish Sea to the west and England to the east, while the rugged Cambrian Mountains cover much of the north. Most people live in the towns and coastal cities of industrial southern Wales.

Welsh culture

Traditional Welsh pastimes have survived and are best preserved in the rural communities of northern Wales. The Welsh love music, and many towns and villages have their own male voice choirs. Choirs compete in *eisteddfods* – musical festivals that celebrate Welsh culture.

Train station in Anglesey

Welsh language
Wales is officially a bilingual country, where both English and Welsh are spoken. Welsh is an ancient Celtic language, spoken by about 20 per cent of the population. Road signs appear in both Welsh and English, and the television channel S4C. broadcasts Welsh-language programmes.

Literature festival
The Welsh love of literature is well-known. The country's strong oral tradition has its roots in the medieval bards (singer-poets). Even today, a poet whose work wins a competition at an *eisteddfod* will be given the title Bard. Every year, an international festival of literature is held in the small town of Hay-on-Wye. Book-lovers from across Britain visit to hear celebrated writers read from their works.

St. David's Day
On March 1, the Welsh honour St. David, their patron saint. David was the 6th-century monk who helped convert Wales to Christianity. He is said to have founded a dozen monasteries. According to tradition, David also turned the leek into a national symbol when he persuaded soldiers to wear leeks in their hats, to distinguish themselves in battle.

St. David

Welsh heritage

The Welsh are descended from the Celts, who withstood the Romans and the Saxons to maintain a separate nation. In 770, the Welsh built a dyke to mark the border between Wales and England. Centuries of cross-border skirmishes followed, until Wales was conquered in the 13th century. The 1535 Act of Union united Wales and England.

Mythology
Early Celtic myths were handed down by word-of-mouth and were later recorded in medieval Welsh manuscripts. In the 19th century, 11 tales were translated into English and collected in the *Mabinogion*. The tales recount magical acts by early Welsh nobility and stories about King Arthur's court.

Two characters from the tale of Branwen

Statue at Harlech castle, Gwynedd

Industrial revolution
During the Industrial Revolution, many people left agriculture to work in coal-mines. After World War II, the mining industry declined. Today, most Welsh people are employed in the manufacturing and service industries.

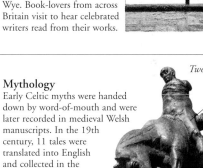

The Welsh Assembly
In a 1997 referendum, the Welsh people voted to have their own government. The National Assembly of Wales sat for the first time in 1999. Its 60 elected members manage an annual budget of £7 billion and control a range of functions – rom education to Welsh language policy.

Rugby
Rugby Union is the national game, and it is followed passionately at both regional and international levels. Each town in the south has its own rugby team. The annual Five Nations tournament, in which the Welsh team competes against England, Ireland, Scotland, and France, is the highlight of the Welsh sporting year.

The Welsh national team wears red.

Welsh castles

Wales is dotted with medieval castles – a legacy of the turbulent years when the Welsh and the English battled for supremacy. The greatest period of construction came after the English king, Edward I, gained control of Wales in 1282. Edward built a chain of magnificent castle-fortresses as secure bases to help him subdue the Welsh people.

Conwy Castle

FIND OUT MORE — CELTS — INDUSTRIAL REVOLUTION — MYTHS AND LEGENDS — UNITED KINGDOM — UNITED KINGDOM, HISTORY OF

WHITE HOUSE

HOME TO EVERY PRESIDENT of the United States since John Adams, the White House is one of the world's best known buildings. Officially known as the Executive Mansion, it is sited at 1600 Pennsylvania Avenue, Washington, D.C. It is both a place of work and a home, with offices for the president and his staff as well as private rooms for the first family.

White House under construction.

First occupants
The first residents of the White House were President John Adams and his wife Abigail. The house was not completed when they arrived – it was unfinished, only six of the rooms were plastered, and the grounds were full of the builders' sheds and equipment. Mrs. Adams had to hang her washing to dry in the East Room.

History of the White House

Some 40 presidents have lived in the White House since it was first built. During its 200-year history, the house has developed from an elegant residence to the headquarters of the ruler of a modern superpower. Built of stone, the building was painted white to hide damage after the War of 1812. It takes 570 gallons of paint to cover the outside walls.

Building of the White House
In 1791 a competition was launched to design a new house for the president of the United States on a site chosen by George Washington. An Irish-American architect called James Hoban won the $500 prize, and work on the new mansion began in October 1791. President John Adams moved in in 1800.

Expansion
In 1814, when Britain and the United States were at war, the White House was burned. It was rebuilt over the next three years, though various additions were made later. President Theodore Roosevelt added the West Wing to provide more office space, in 1902, and the East Wing was built in 1942.

Inside the White House

The White House has 132 rooms arranged on four floors (two public floors and two for the first family) and two basements. There are 32 bathrooms, a cinema, a gymnasium, and seven staircases. Apart from the Oval Office, the most famous parts of the building are the historic reception rooms in the central section.

Entrance Hall

The Green Room has been used for many purposes – it has been a sitting room, dining room, and even a place for playing cards.

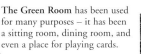

White House (back view)

The Cross Hall, with its elegant classical columns, connects the Entrance Hall with many of the White House's main rooms.

The State Dining Room, with its round tables, can seat up to 140 guests for formal dinners.

The Map Room is now a meeting room for the president and first lady. President Franklin Roosevelt followed the progress of World War II from this room.

The East Room is used for public gatherings, from dances to award presentations. The bodies of seven presidents, from Lincoln to John F. Kennedy, have lain in state here.

The library contains a collection of books designed to cover the full range of American thought and literature. The room also contains volumes of presidential papers.

Oval Office
Situated in the West Wing, the Oval Office is where the president works and meets heads of state and other important visitors. The decoration and furniture reflect each president's personal taste, but the presidential seal on the carpet and the flags behind the desk always remain.

The Blue Room is an oval-shaped reception room. It is sumptuously decorated in the French Empire style.

China Room

The Diplomatic Reception Room forms an entrance for the presidential family and for ambassadors arriving to visit the President.

Tourists
Around 1.5 million people visit the White House every year. They are attracted by the beautiful interiors, as well as the house's historical importance. Since the interior was restored in 1948, each first lady has added furnishings and ornaments appropriate for its early-19th century style.

| FIND OUT MORE | AMERICAN REVOLUTION | ARCHITECTURE | UNITED STATES OF AMERICA | UNITED STATES, HISTORY OF | WASHINGTON, GEORGE |

ZULUS

THE ZULUS ARE ONE OF THE largest groups of Bantu-speaking peoples in South Africa, with a population of about 7 million. They live in Kwazulu-Natal, one of the country's nine provinces. Zulu is one of the country's nine official languages. The Zulu people were originally peaceful farmers, but in the early 1800s they formed the strongest military force in the country.

Zulu country

Under British rule, Zululand formed the northeastern part of Natal Province, which lies along the coast with the Indian Ocean. The present province of Kwazulu-Natal covers a much larger area. Zulus form about 82 per cent of its population.

Zulu history

The ancestors of the Zulus came to Natal from West Africa in the late 1600s. They were organized into a powerful people by Shaka, who made himself king of the Zulus in 1818. Britain annexed Natal in 1879, and crushed the Zulus in a bloody battle at Ulundi. Zululand became part of Natal in 1897.

Leaders

Shaka was an aggressive leader. Under his successor, Dingane, the Zulus fought a brutal war with the Boers in 1838. Dingane's successor Mpande surrendered control of much of Zululand. His son Cetshwayo led the Zulus in the Anglo-Zulu war of 1879. Cetshwayo annihilated a British force at Isandlwana, but was defeated by the British at Ulundi in 1883.

Cetshwayo

Inkatha movement

In 1975 Chief Mangosuthu Gatsha Buthelezi – the head of the Kwazulu homeland – revived a movement called Inkatha. This organization was founded in the 1920s to promote Zulu culture. Buthelezi turned it into a political party dedicated to gaining Zulu independence.

Women

Each of a man's wives is the boss of her own home. By tradition, women grow crops, while men hunt or look after the animals. Many Zulu women now work as nurses or teachers in the towns and cities.

Ways of life

The king, a descendant of Cetshwayo, is the head of the Zulu clans. A clan is formed of several villages, each containing a number of *imzi* (groups of homesteads). Agriculture is the basis of the Zulu economy. Farmers grow vegetables and grain, and rear cattle, goats, and sheep. Many men labour in South Africa's industries and mines.

Being a skilled stick-fighter is part of Zulu manhood.

Religion

Many Zulus still follow their ancient religion, which is based on ancestor worship. The supreme god is Nkulunkulu, the maker of all things. More than half of the Zulus are Christians. Others belong to a Zionist Spirit church that believes in faith healing. Traditional Zulu practitioners deal with illnesses that are believed to be supernatural in origin.

Marriage

A Zulu man may have several wives, but marriage between members of the same clan is discouraged. The bridegroom has to give his bride's family *lobolo* (bride wealth) as compensation for their loss. Wedding ceremonies are elaborate, with dancing, singing, and the presentation of gifts by the bride's party.

Cultural heritage

Zulus are proud of their culture and maintain their ancient traditions. From boyhood, men are trained in the art of stick-fighting. Most men tend to carry a stick or an umbrella when they go out, even in the towns. Zulus perform traditional dances at ceremonial occasions, such as weddings and coming-of-age celebrations.

Crafts

Women are skilled at beadwork. In the past, beads were made of ivory, clay, or bone. The use of mass-produced beads of glass or plastic allows the women to spend more time on design. Potters make simple clay vessels for different uses. Metal-workers produce a variety of tools and weapons.

Beaded necklet

Buffalo thorn symbolizes the ancestral spirits.

Death

Zulus believe that illness and death are caused by witchcraft. They think that a dead person's spirit roams outside its *kraal* (village), causing trouble. A *sangoma* (diviner) is asked to call the spirit home, through the sacrifice of an animal and rituals to purify the *kraal*. Once this is done, the spirit is regarded as being at rest.

FIND OUT MORE

RELIGION   SOUTH AFRICA   SOUTH AFRICA, HISTORY OF

BIOGRAPHIES

Muhammad Ali
b. 1942

Boxer Muhammad Ali, original name Cassius Clay, was born in Louisville, Kentucky. At the age of 18, he won a gold medal at the Rome Olympics, and, after turning professional, he won the world heavyweight title in 1964, defeating the towering Sonny Liston. The young Ali was a great entertainer in the ring, his inimitable boxing style fitting his own phrase: "Float like a butterfly, sting like a bee". He courted controversy, both through immodest references to himself as "the greatest", and through his political and religious views. He joined the Black Muslims organization in 1964 and adopted the name Ali. In 1967, after refusing to be drafted into the army for service in the Vietnam War, Ali was stripped of his title and sentenced to prison. Cleared by the Supreme Court in 1970, he returned to the ring, and retook the world title in 1974, beating George Foreman in Zaire (Congo) – the famous "rumble in the jungle". He lost and regained the title again in 1978, becoming the first heavyweight to win the world championship three times. After his retirement in 1981, Ali endured physical decline through Parkinson's disease. As a sign of respect for one of the world's great sporting personalities, he was invited to light the flame opening the 1996 Olympic games at Atlanta, Georgia.

ALI'S GREATEST FIGHTS

February 1964 Beats Sonny Liston to become world heavyweight champion.

May 1965 Knocks out Liston in just 48 seconds to retain the world title.

November 1965 Successfully defends his title against former world champion Floyd Patterson.

March 1971 Fails in bid to retake the world title, losing on points to the champion, Joe Frazier.

October 1974 Regains the world title by knocking out George Foreman in Kinshasa, Zaire (Congo).

October 1975 Retains his title, defeating Joe Frazier in a punishing bout in Manila, Philippines – the fight is known as the "thrilla in Manila".

September 1978 Wins the world title for the third time at the age of 36, defeating Leon Spinks on points.

Yasser Arafat
b. 1929

Palestinian leader Yasser Arafat was once widely condemned as a terrorist. In the 1960s and 1970s, his *Al Fatah* organization played a leading role in Palestinian attacks on Israel and its supporters worldwide. As leader of the Palestine Liberation Organization (PLO), however, Arafat came to favour negotiation rather than armed struggle. A peace agreement with Israel in 1993 provided for the creation of an autonomous Palestinian government in the Israeli-occupied territories of the West Bank and Gaza. Arafat was awarded the Nobel Peace Prize in 1994, together with Israeli leaders Shimon Peres and Yitzhak Rabin. In 1996, Arafat was elected president of the first Palestinian government in the former Israeli-occupied territories.

Arafat has retained a distinctively Arab style of dress throughout his career.

PLO

After the creation of the state of Israel in Palestine in 1948, the Palestinian Arabs had no country of their own. Many thousands of Palestinians lived in refugee camps around Israel's borders. In 1967, Israel took over the West Bank of the Jordan and the Gaza Strip – areas with large Palestinian populations. These "occupied territories" became the focus for a campaign to create a Palestinian Arab state. At first, the Palestine Liberation Organization (PLO), headed by Yasser Arafat, called for the complete destruction of Israel.

Peace process

The Israelis were too strong to be overcome by terrorism or war. In the 1980s, the Palestinian people in the occupied territories began a general uprising against Israeli rule, known as the *Intifada*. Acts of resistance, including riots and strikes, made the areas impossible to control. In 1993, Israel agreed to allow the Palestinians to govern themselves. In return, the PLO agreed to accept the existence of Israel. Despite opposition from extremists on both sides, the peace agreement was implemented and Palestinian self-rule began in 1996.

Giorgio Armani
b. 1935

Italian clothes designer Giorgio Armani worked as a window dresser in a department store before joining the men's clothing company Cerruti as a designer in 1961. He established his own fashion consultancy in Milan in 1974, and quickly gained widespread renown as a designer of smart menswear. Armani specialized in a relaxed style based on elegant textures and simple outlines. Armani suits, in particular, became a byword for understated chic during the 1980s. He also diversified into womenswear, featuring loose-fitting jackets and smart but unfussy trousers. Among the other specialities for which he is known are culottes for women and leather jackets.

Models wear Armani leather jackets during a fashion shoot.

Louis Armstrong
1901–71

Louis "Satchmo" Armstrong ranks among the greatest figures in the history of jazz. Born in New Orleans, he was brought up in extreme poverty and played the trumpet for a living while still in his teens. By 1923, when he moved to Chicago and made his first recordings with King Oliver's Creole Jazz Band, he was already acknowledged as the top jazz trumpeter of his time. He was soon well known for his original "scat" singing style. Fronting various big bands in the 1930s and 1940s, he became a world-famous entertainer. In 1947, he returned to playing with a small combo, the Louis Armstrong All Stars. In his later years, he had huge success as the singer of the hit singles "Hello Dolly" and "What a Wonderful World".

SELECTED RECORDINGS

1923 "Chimes Blues", King Oliver's Creole Jazz Band

1926 "Heebie Jeebies", The Hot Five

1927 "Potato Head Blues", The Hot Seven

1929 "Ain't Misbehavin'", Louis Armstrong & His Orchestra

1931 "Walkin' My Baby Back Home", Louis Armstrong & His Orchestra

1936 "On the Sunny Side of the Street", Louis Armstrong & His Orchestra

1955 "Mack the Knife", Louis Armstrong All Stars

1963 "Hello Dolly", Louis Armstrong All Stars

1968 "What a Wonderful World"

1969 "All the Time in the World"

Arthur Ashe
1943–93

Born in Richmond, Virginia, Arthur Ashe was the first African-American to become a top player in men's tennis. He was selected for the US Davis Cup team in 1963, at the age of 19. After being drafted into the army for two years, he returned to tennis in 1968 and immediately won his first Grand Slam singles title at the US Open. His crowning triumph came in 1975, when he won the men's singles championship at Wimbledon in a thrilling final against reigning champion Jimmy Connors. Ashe was noted for his quiet, graceful style of play. After retiring from tennis in 1980, he was put in charge of the US Davis Cup squad. He died at the age of 50, having been infected with HIV, the AIDS virus, from a blood transfusion.

KEY CAREER DATES

1963 First represents the United States in the Davis Cup.

1968 Wins the US Open men's singles championship.

1969 Turns professional.

1970 Wins the Australian Open men's singles title.

1974 Elected president of the ATP (Association of Tennis Professionals).

1975 Wins the Wimbledon men's singles title.

1981 Selected as captain of the US Davis Cup team.

Amitabh Bachchan
b. 1942

Indian film star Amitabh Bachchan is the son of the Hindu poet Harishchandra Bachchan. He was a stage actor and radio announcer before moving into cinema in the late 1960s. During the 1970s, his role as an "angry young man" in *Zanjeer*, and as a rebel vigilante in many other hit movies, established him as the biggest movie star that the Hindi film industry had ever produced. Bachchan married the noted actress Jaya Bhaduri and, in 1995, founded the controversial entertainment conglomerate ABCL (Amitabh Bachchan Corporation Ltd).

Bachchan in a scene from *Sholay*

Jane Austen
1775–1817

The English novelist Jane Austen lived most of her short life in Hampshire, the county of her birth. Her father was a rector, and she inhabited the small world of country gentry in which all her books are set. Austen completed the first version of her most famous novel, *Pride and Prejudice*, in 1797, but she did not publish a book until 1811, when *Sense and Sensibility* appeared. *Northanger Abbey* and *Persuasion* were published after her death. Her work applies keen wit and sharp observation to problems of love, marriage, and women's position in a male-dominated society. It proves that literature dealing with "domestic" issues can be great.

JANE AUSTEN'S NOVELS	
1811	*Sense and Sensibility*
1813	*Pride and Prejudice*
1814	*Mansfield Park*
1816	*Emma*
1818	*Northanger Abbey*
1818	*Persuasion*

Christiaan Neethling Barnard
b. 1922

The renowned heart surgeon Christiaan Barnard was born in Beaufort West, South Africa, and studied medicine in Cape Town. After further study in the United States, Barnard returned to Cape Town to work at Groote Schuur Hospital, where he began to perform heart transplant experiments on dogs. In 1967, he performed what is normally regarded as the first successful human heart transplant. A terminally ill patient, 53-year-old Louis Washkansky, received a heart from a 25-year-old woman who had died in a car crash. Washkansky died 18 days later, from pneumonia. Barnard went on to achieve what might more properly be considered the first successful heart transplant in January 1968. The patient, Philip Blaiberg, lived for a year and a half after the operation. By the time Barnard retired from surgery in 1983, some of his patients had survived for several years.

Thomas Barnardo
1845–1905

Irish philanthropist Thomas Barnardo was born in Dublin, the son of a furrier. When he was 21, he left Ireland to study medicine in London, intending to go to China as a missionary doctor when he qualified. He soon gave up this plan, turning instead to helping poor families in London's East End. He raised money to provide homeless children with a place to sleep, and trained them to do jobs such as chopping wood, polishing boots, and making brushes. During his lifetime, more than 50,000 children, some handicapped, were sheltered and trained in "Dr. Barnardo's Homes". Today, the work of the charity includes finding foster homes for children, helping with adoption, and supporting families of children with mental and physical disabilities.

BECKET DATES

1155 Appointed chancellor by King Henry II.

1162 Appointed archbishop of Canterbury.

1164 Earns the king's disfavour for upholding the independence of the Church.

1170 Returns from exile to Canterbury, but is killed on the king's orders.

1173 Proclaimed a saint (canonized) by Pope Alexander III.

1174 Henry II is obliged to perform penance at St. Thomas's tomb.

Becket's tomb at Canterbury was soon associated with miracles, and became a place of pilgrimage. It was the destination of the travellers in Chaucer's Canterbury Tales.

St. Thomas Becket
1118–70

Thomas Becket was the son of a merchant. He became a close friend of the English king, Henry II (1133–89), who appointed him chancellor, the most powerful position in the land below the king himself. Becket served Henry loyally, and in 1162 the king made him archbishop of Canterbury, expecting that he would continue to be a faithful servant. As archbishop, however, Becket resisted all the king's attempts to bring the Church under royal control. In 1170, frustrated and furious, Henry cried out, "Will no one rid me of this turbulent priest?" Four knights, taking the king at his word, rode to Canterbury and murdered Becket in front of the altar. After his violent death, for which Henry repented, he was proclaimed a saint and his tomb became a place of pilgrimage.

Tony Blair
b. 1953

POLITICAL CAREER

1975 Joins the Labour Party.

1983 Becomes member of parliament for the Sedgefield constituency.

1988 Elected to the Labour shadow cabinet.

1994 Elected leader of the Labour Party.

1997 Becomes prime minister after a landslide general election victory.

British prime minister since 1997, Tony Blair was born and brought up in Edinburgh, Scotland. At Oxford University in the 1970s, he was lead singer of a rock band called Ugly Rumours. He became a lawyer, but after marrying Cherie Booth in 1980, he decided to enter politics. Blair became a Labour member of parliament in 1983 and soon made his mark in the House of Commons. In July 1994, he was elected Labour leader and embarked on a transformation of the party's policies. Abandoning traditional left-wing ideas, Blair's New Labour triumphed in the 1997 general election. Despite criticism in the press, during his first two years in office Blair remained popular with British voters.

Tony Blair became Britain's youngest prime minister for 185 years when he was elected in 1997.

Death of Brian Boru

Louis Braille
1809–52

French educationalist Louis Braille was born near Paris, France. Blind from the age of three, he entered the Paris Institute for Blind Youth when he was 10 years old. He studied the organ and became a teacher at the institute in 1826. Three years later, Braille published the first account of a system of raised-dot writing that would enable the blind to read by touch. By 1837, he had perfected his invention, and the Braille system of writing has since changed the lives of millions of blind people throughout the world.

Brian Boru
926–1014

Brian Boru, or Borumha, was the first person to unite Ireland under a single ruler. After becoming king of Munster, in southwest Ireland, in 976, he gradually extended his rule over the rest of the island. By 1002, he was acknowledged as High King of Ireland. He governed his new kingdom wisely, in collaboration with the Catholic Church, but revolt broke out in the Viking-dominated east of the country in 1013. Boru met the Viking confederation in battle at Clontarf in the following year. Although his army was victorious, Boru was killed in the battle. After his death, Ireland quickly split apart once more into squabbling kingdoms.

Reading Braille
Braille consists of a different pattern of raised dots for each letter of the alphabet. For example, A is represented by one dot, B is two dots one above the other, C is two dots side by side, and so on. The numbers are formed by preceding the signs for the letters A to J with a special "number sign". Braille readers are taught to touch the dots with their right hand while searching for the start of the next line of the text with their left.

Don Bradman
b. 1908

Australian batsman Donald Bradman was the most consistent run-scorer in the history of cricket. As a boy in the country town of Bowral, he practised playing cricket on his own with just a golf ball and a cricket stump. He scored 118 on his debut for New South Wales in 1927, and on average hit a century once in every three innings for the rest of his career. He played his first test for Australia in 1928 and captained the team from 1936. His ability to accumulate runs in tests was quite unparalleled. In the 1930 series against England, he made scores of 334, 254, and 232. His career was interrupted by World War II, but he returned to cricket in 1946 with his abilities barely impaired. His test average would have topped 100 if he had not been bowled out for a duck in his last test innings in 1948. In 1949, Bradman was knighted for his contribution to cricket.

Don Bradman was only 1 m 70 cm (5 ft 7 in) tall, dwarfed by his 1934 opening partner Bill Woodfull.

CAREER STATISTICS

Total runs scored 28,067

Career average 95.14

Number of centuries 117

Number of double centuries 37

Highest score 452 not out, New South Wales v Queensland, 1929/30

Test appearances 52

Test runs scored 6,996

Test average 99.94

Number of test centuries 29

Highest test score 334 v England at Headingley, 1930

Highest total runs in a test series 974 (average 139.14) against England in 1930

Total runs scored in Sheffield Shield 8,896 (average 109.82)

Al Capone
1899–1947

Alphonse "Scarface" Capone grew up amid the violence and poverty of New York's Brooklyn district. He dropped out of school early and joined various gangs, receiving a knife-wound to the cheek that earned him his nickname. In 1919 he moved to Chicago, where he ran brothels and gambling dens, and traded in "bootleg" alcohol, made illegal by Prohibition. By 1925, he was in control of much of Chicago's flourishing criminal underworld, dealing ruthlessly with other mobsters who stood in his way. His yearly profits were estimated at between $60 million and $165 million, money used freely to bribe local police and politicians. Capone successfully avoided prosecution for his many violent crimes, but in 1931 a federal court sentenced him to 11 years in jail for tax evasion. He emerged from prison a broken man. Capone was unrepentant about his life of crime, saying, "All I ever did was to sell whiskey to our best people."

The St. Valentine's Day Massacre
On 14 February 1929 – St. Valentine's Day – a particularly brutal gangland slaying took place in a beer warehouse in Chicago. Seven members of the gang run by Bugsy Moran were gunned down by killers dressed in police uniforms. This detail appears to have especially outraged Chicago police chief William Russell, who declared a "war to the finish" against organized crime in the city. The public demanded that someone be brought to justice for the killings. The investigation soon focused on Al Capone, who was widely believed to have ordered the massacre. Capone had made sure he was on vacation at the time, and nothing could be proved against him. But the demand for action by the authorities led directly to his subsequent prosecution and conviction for tax evasion.

Anders Celsius
1701–44

Anders Celsius was professor of astronomy at the University of Uppsala, Sweden, and built an observatory there in 1740. He is most famous, however, for the temperature scale associated with his name. He presented this idea to the Swedish Academy of Sciences in 1742, describing a thermometer that had 0° as the boiling point of water and 100° as the temperature at which water froze. Within a few years of his death, other scientists began using this scale, but with the freezing and boiling points reversed.

Subrahmanyan Chandrasekhar
1910–1995

Astrophysicist Subrahmanyan Chandrasekhar was born in British-ruled India, in the city of Lahore, now in Pakistan. He was inspired to become a scientist by the example of his uncle, Sir Chandrasekhara Venkata Raman, who won the Nobel Prize for physics in 1930. Chandrasekhar studied at Presidency College, Madras, and Cambridge University, England, before moving to the United States to work at the Univeristy of Chicago in 1936. He specialized in the study of small, dense stars known as white dwarfs. He was responsible for the observation that stars above a certain size would never become white dwarfs, and this size boundary is known as the Chandrasekhar limit. He was awarded the 1983 Nobel Prize for physics jointly with William Fowler.

A group of 1983 Nobel Prize winners

William Fowler

Subrahmanyan Chandrasekhar

Bill Clinton
b. 1946

The 42nd president of the United States, Bill Clinton made his political reputation as governor of Arkansas, a position he held with only two years' interruption from 1978 to 1992. He won nomination as the 1992 Democratic presidential candidate despite having to admit that he had been unfaithful to his wife, Hillary. His victory over President George Bush, a Republican, and Independent Ross Perot ended 12 years of Republican rule. Although Clinton's liberal reform programme soon ran into trouble, he presided over a striking economic recovery and was comfortably re-elected in 1996, defeating the Republican candidate, Bob Dole. In 1998, after admitting to an affair with White House aide Monica Lewinsky, he became only the second US president to be impeached by Congress. However, the Senate failed to remove him from office largely because he remained popular with the majority of Americans.

Changing president
Bill Clinton was elected US president in 1992, promising to bring in liberal reforms after the conservative era of his predecessors, Ronald Reagan and George Bush. However, after the success of conservative Republicans in mid-term elections in 1994, Clinton adopted many of the policies previously advocated by his opponents, such as cutting federal spending on welfare payments.

Actress Lya Lys kisses a statue's foot in a scene from *L'Age d'Or*.

Salvador Dali
1904–89

Salvador Dali was an artist as famous for his eccentric lifestyle as for his works. Born in Catalonia, Spain, he moved to France in 1928 and joined the Surrealist movement. He became one of the leading painters in the Surrealist style, which placed familiar images in unfamiliar situations, creating dreamlike and disturbing effects. Dali's gift for self-publicity soon made him the most famous representative of the movement. One of his most memorable stunts occurred in 1936, when he turned up for the opening of the London Surrealist exhibition in a diving suit. The following year he was expelled from the Surrealist movement, chiefly because of his support for the Francoist side in the Spanish Civil War (1936–39). Dali moved to the United States in 1940, finally returning to Spain in 1955. In his later years he became a Catholic and adopted a more academic style of painting. His standing as an artist is much disputed, but his fame is unquestionable.

Dali at the movies
In 1929, Salvador Dali collaborated with Spanish film director Luis Buñuel on a 24-minute movie they called *Un chien andalou* (*An Andalusian Dog*). It consisted of a sequence of unrelated incidents, including a hand being eaten by ants and an eyeball being slashed by a razor. The following year Dali and Buñuel worked together again on *L'Age d'or* (*The Golden Age*), an almost equally bizarre 60-minute film in which two lovers are repeatedly interrupted by the arrival of policemen and priests. The movie met with violent abuse from some cinema audiences.

WORKS BY DALI

1929 Painting: *The Accommodation of Desire*

1929 Film (with Luis Buñuel): *Un chien andalou*

1930 Film (with Luis Buñuel): *L'Age d'or*

1931 Painting: *The Persistence of Memory*

1937 Painting: *Sleep*

1942 Autobiography: *The Secret Life of Salvador Dali*

1944 Novel: *Hidden Faces*

1945 Dream sequences for Alfred Hitchcock's film *Spellbound*

1951 Painting: *Christ of St. John of the Cross*

Diana, Princess of Wales
1961–97

Diana, Princess of Wales, was born the Honourable Diana Spencer at Sandringham, Norfolk. The daughter of an earl, she was suddenly thrust into the limelight in February 1981 when she became engaged to Charles, Prince of Wales. Their spectacular royal wedding in July of that year was watched by millions of people around the world. Diana and Charles had two children, but their marriage soon ran into difficulties. They were separated in 1992 and divorced four years later. After the separation, Diana built an independent life that won her the admiration of many young women. Her glamorous appearances at prominent social events made her the most photographed woman in the world. She also worked strenuously for a range of charitable causes, notably on behalf of children and AIDS sufferers. Diana often found the immense media interest that she attracted unwelcome, especially when it was focused upon her troubled private life. In the months before her death, she became involved with Dodi Fayed, the son of Harrod's owner Mohamed Al Fayed. Diana and Dodi were killed in a car crash in Paris on 31 August 1997, while being pursued by press photographers on motorbikes. Diana's funeral a week later was an occasion of intense emotion. She was buried at Althorp House, the Spencer family home in Northamptonshire.

Mine campaigner
Shortly before her death, Diana became involved in the campaign for a world-wide ban on the use of landmines. She visited Angola and Bosnia, two countries ravaged by the effect of mines, meeting people who had lost limbs in landmine accidents. The publicity her presence brought to the campaign was partly responsible for 90 nations signing a treaty to ban landmines a month after her death. Later that same year the International Campaign to Ban Land-mines won the 1997 Nobel Peace Prize.

Diana's children
Diana had two sons, Prince William (above right), born in 1982, and Prince Harry, born in 1984. They are second and third in line to the British throne, after their father, Prince Charles. Both boys were sent to Eton College for their formal education. Despite appeals for the media to respect their privacy in the wake of their mother's death, they were much in the public eye, especially William, who became a teen idol in North America.

Bartolomeu Dias
1450–1500

Bartolomeu Dias (or Diaz) was one of the Portuguese navigators who explored the sea route from Europe to India in the late 1400s. Nothing is known about his early life, but at some point he travelled to the court of the kingdom of Aragon, where he learned the latest scientific views about the geography of the Earth. In 1486, Dias was instructed by Portugal's King John II to find out if it was possible to sail around Africa. The following year he sailed south, following the West African coast, until a storm blew his ships out of sight of land. After 13 days at sea, he turned north and was amazed to see land on his left. He had rounded Africa's southern Cape of Good Hope without realizing it. The way to India lay open. Dias, however, turned back to report to his king. The first voyage to India was made by Vasco da Gama ten years later. In 1500, Dias sailed in Pedro Cabral's fleet that landed by accident in Brazil. Later on the same voyage, he was lost at sea while rounding the cape that he had discovered.

PORTUGUESE VOYAGES

1434 Encouraged by Portugal's Prince Henry the Navigator, Gil Eannes sails beyond Cape Bojador, on the northwest coast of Africa.

1444 Portuguese sailor Dinis Dias sails south down the coast of Africa to the mouth of the Senegal River.

1487 Bartolomeu Dias rounds the Cape of Good Hope, the southern tip of Africa.

1497–98 Vasco da Gama sails with a fleet of three vessels around the Cape of Good Hope and across the Indian Ocean to Calicut on the west coast of India.

1500 A fleet captained by Pedro Alvarez Cabral lands on the coast of Brazil and claims the territory for the Portuguese crown.

1519–21 Portuguese sailor Ferdinand Magellan leads the first expedition to sail around the globe. He does not complete the voyage, dying in the Philippines.

Joe DiMaggio
1914–99

Born in Martinez, California, Joseph Paul DiMaggio began his baseball career in 1932 in the Pacific Coast League. He joined the New York Yankees in 1936 and remained with them until his retirement in 1951. An outstanding outfielder and powerful hitter, he was known by the nicknames "Joltin Joe" and "The Yankee Clipper". DiMaggio was voted Most Valuable Player (MVP) three times and twice won the batting championship, in 1939 and 1940. He holds the record for scoring a hit in 56 consecutive games, in 1941. In 1954 he married his second wife, the film star Marilyn Monroe. Although the marriage lasted only a short time, the two stars remained friends up to Monroe's death.

The 1947 New Look introduced long, full skirts.

Christian Dior
1905–57

French fashion designer Christian Dior was born in the small town of Granville, Normandy. He learned his trade at the Piguet and LeLong fashion houses in the 1930s. After World War II, he founded his own fashion house and achieved a meteoric rise to fame with his first collection, the 1947 New Look. A reaction against the austerity of the war years, the New Look brought in tight waists, padded hips, long, full skirts, and high heels to create an elegant, feminine look full of glamour. Dior said, "It was because women longed to be women again that they adopted the New Look." In the 1950s, stylistic innovations such as the A-line, with narrow shoulders and a flared skirt, and the Sack dress or chemise kept Dior at the forefront of the fashion world.

Gustave Eiffel
1832–1923

French engineer Gustave Eiffel was a pioneer of the use of iron as material for large-scale building. After graduating from the College of Art and Manufacturing in 1855, he specialized in bridge construction. He directed the building of an iron bridge in Bordeaux in 1858, followed by further spectacular bridges over the Douro River at Porto, Portugal, and over the Truyère River in southern France. The bridge over the Truyère, known as the Garabit Viaduct, had an arch spanning 162 m (540 ft), and was in its time the highest bridge in the world. Eiffel also designed the metal frameworks for the Bon Marché department store in Paris and for the Statue of Liberty in New York. But he really came to the world's attention for his construction of the Eiffel Tower for the 1889 Paris Exhibition.

Building the Eiffel Tower
The tower took two years to build. It has 2.5 million rivets and 18,000 steel pieces. At 300.5 m (986 ft), it was the tallest building in the world until 1930. Intended as a temporary structure to be dismantled when the exhibition finished, the tower has proved astonishingly durable.

Alexander Fleming in his laboratory, 1943.

Sir Alexander Fleming
1881–1955

Scottish bacteriologist Alexander Fleming was born on a farm in rural Ayrshire. He qualified as a surgeon at St. Mary's hospital in London, and spent his whole career there, apart from a spell as a medical officer in France during World War I. Fleming became a researcher in the hospital's bacteriological laboratory. He pioneered the use of salvarsan against syphilis and discovered the antiseptic powers of lysozyme, present in tears and mucus. In 1928, quite by chance, he noticed a curious mould, penicillin, growing on a bacteria culture. He found penicillin to have extraordinary antibiotic powers, but was unable to exploit his discovery. Eleven years later, the researchers Howard Florey and Ernst Chain perfected a method for producing penicillin, in time for it to save thousands of lives during World War II. Fleming shared the 1945 Nobel Prize for medicine with Florey and Chain.

Dame Margot Fonteyn
1919–91

English ballet dancer Margot Fonteyn was born Margaret Hookham in Reigate, Surrey. She first studied dance while living in Shanghai, China, with her parents. On her return to England, she joined the Vic-Wells Ballet, which later became the Sadler's Wells Ballet, and then the Royal Ballet. She stayed with the company throughout her long career. Her exceptional talent was quickly recognized and she became a prima ballerina. She excelled in the great classical ballets such as *Swan Lake* and *The Sleeping Beauty*, but choreographers Sir Frederick Ashton and Ninette de Valois also created several new ballets for her. In 1962, her career reached new heights when she began her famous partnership with the Russian dancer Rudolf Nureyev. Fonteyn is widely regarded as one of the best dancers of her time, renowned for her technical skill and characterizations. She helped to popularize ballet in Britain and her world tours established her as an international star.

KEY CAREER DATES

1934 Joins the Vic-Wells ballet company.

1935 Becomes prima ballerina at the Vic-Wells.

1946 Dances in Sir Frederick Ashton's *Symphonic Variations*.

1956 Becomes a Dame of the British Empire.

1962 Performs for the first time with Russian dancer Rudolf Nureyev.

St. Francis of Assisi
1181–1226

The future St. Francis was born Giovanni Bernadone, the son of a silk merchant in Assisi, central Italy. Until the age of 21, he devoted himself to pleasure, but then turned to religion after a long illness. Choosing a life of poverty, he began to preach and care for the sick, surviving by begging for alms. He soon attracted a handful of followers, who settled in Assisi. In 1210, Pope Innocent II gave official approval to the group, who were called the Friars Minor. They were the seed from which the Franciscan order was to grow. In 1223, Francis travelled to Egypt, where he preached in front of the sultan. Returning to Europe, he is alleged to have received the stigmata – the marks of the wounds of the crucified Christ. He was proclaimed a saint two years after his death. Francis is now remembered above all for his legendary kindness to animals.

Earthquake damage at Assisi, 1997

The Basilica di San Francesco
In 1228, two years after St. Francis's death, the Franciscans began construction of a religious building in Assisi to house his remains. The walls of this magnificent basilica were decorated by the greatest artists of the early Italian Renaissance, including Giotto, Cimabue, and Simone Martini. It has remained a centre of pilgrimage up to the present day. In 1997, however, the basilica suffered severe earthquake damage. Some of the famous frescoes were completely destroyed.

Clark Gable
1901–60

William Clark Gable was the son of an Ohio oil driller. He began work in a factory at the age of 14 and went on to a variety of casual jobs while trying to break into acting. Growing success on the stage late in the 1920s earned him a Hollywood screen test, but he was turned down by producer Darryl F. Zanuck, who said, "His ears are too big." In 1931, however, he began to land major movie roles, culminating in an Oscar-winning appearance in *It Happened One Night* (1934). He rapidly developed into the most popular leading man in cinema and was dubbed "the King of Hollywood". By the time he starred as Rhett Butler in the epic *Gone with the Wind* (1939), he was at the peak of his career. Gable's third wife, the actress Carole Lombard, was killed in an air crash in 1942, and the bereaved actor joined the wartime air force. After the war, he never regained his former popularity, although his last movie, *The Misfits*, was one of his best.

Clark Gable with Vivien Leigh in *Gone with the Wind*

Indira Gandhi
1917–84

Indira Gandhi was the daughter of Jawaharlal Nehru, the first prime minister of independent India. She played an active role in the campaign for independence from British rule in the 1940s, enduring a spell in prison. After independence, she served as her father's aide and rose through the upper ranks of the Congress party. In 1966, two years after her father's death, she herself became India's prime minister. In 1975, following her conviction for electoral malpractice, she declared a state of emergency, jailing opponents and passing laws that limited personal freedom. This led to her sound defeat in the national elections of 1977. However, Mrs Gandhi made a remarkable comeback after being acquitted of corruption charges, returning to power in 1980. She was assassinated four years later.

Rajiv Gandhi

Mrs Gandhi's funeral pyre

Death by assassination
Indira Gandhi was assassinated on 31 October 1984 by one of her Sikh bodyguards, in protest at an assault by Indian troops on the Golden Temple at Amritsar, the Sikhs' holiest shrine. After Mrs Gandhi's death, her son, Rajiv, succeeded her as prime minister, but in 1991, he too was assassinated.

George Gershwin
1898–1937

American composer George Gershwin was born in Brooklyn, New York, the son of Russian Jewish immigrants. As a child, he learned to play the piano and taught himself composition. He started to write popular songs in his teens. In the 1920s, he leapt to fame as a writer of Broadway musicals, usually with lyrics by his brother Ira (1896–1983). In 1924 he wrote *Rhapsody in Blue*, the first of his more "serious" pieces. He also wrote a piano concerto and the orchestral suite *An American in Paris*. His major achievement was to bridge the gap between popular and classical music, which he did most effectively in his last great work, the "American folk opera" *Porgy and Bess*.

George Gershwin wrote the music.

Ira Gershwin wrote the lyrics.

GERSHWIN HITS

1924 *Lady Be Good*, musical comedy, including the song "Fascinating Rhythm"

1924 *Rhapsody in Blue*, suite for piano and orchestra

1925 *Concerto in F*, concerto for piano and orchestra

1928 *An American in Paris*, orchestral suite

1930 *Girl Crazy*, musical comedy, including the song "I Got Rhythm"

1931 *Of Thee I Sing*, the first musical comedy to win a Pulitzer Prize

1935 *Porgy and Bess*, folk opera, including the songs "Summertime" and "It Ain't Necesarily So"

Jean-Luc Godard
b. 1930

French film director Jean-Luc Godard first made his name as a film critic in Paris in the 1950s, writing for the influential magazine *Cahiers du Cinéma*. In 1960 he showed his first feature film, *A Bout de Souffle* (*Breathless*). His use of improvised dialogue, disjointed storylines, and unconventional editing techniques instantly established him as a leader of what was dubbed "New Wave" cinema. Godard became increasingly involved in left-wing politics, and by the end of the 1960s was making "revolutionary" films that rejected all traces of commercial cinema. In the 1980s, however, he returned to a more accessible style with movies such as *Passion* (1982). Godard's films have rarely had popular appeal, but he remains an influential figure in the contemporary cinema.

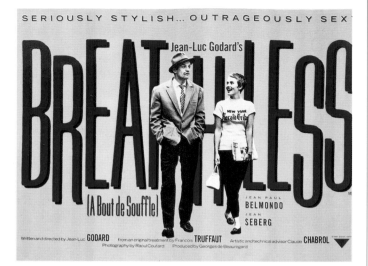

SERIOUSLY STYLISH... OUTRAGEOUSLY SEX

Jean-Luc Godard's

BREATHLESS

(A Bout de Souffle)

JEAN PAUL BELMONDO
JEAN SEBERG

Written and directed by Jean-Luc GODARD from an original treatment by François TRUFFAUT Artistic and technical advisor Claude CHABROL
Photography by Raoul Coutard Produced by Georges de Beauregard

Breathless pair
Godard's first, and most popular, movie was *A Bout de Souffle* (*Breathless*), made in 1959 and released the following year. Filmed on a shoestring budget, it starred an unknown French actor, Jean-Paul Belmondo, and the American actress Jean Seberg. Belmondo plays a gangster on the run who becomes involved with the bookish Seberg. The movie's first audiences were struck less by the flimsy drama, however, than by the director's film techniques, especially the use of the jump-cut, a radical break with the conventions of screen editing.

KEY GODARD MOVIES

1960	*A Bout de Souffle* (*Breathless*)
1963	*Le Mépris* (*Contempt*)
1964	*Bande á Part* (*Band of Outsiders*)
1965	*Alphaville*
1965	*Pierrot le Fou*
1967	*Week-End*
1982	*Passion*
1983	*Prénom: Carmen* (*First Name Carmen*)

Che Guevara
1928–67

Ernesto "Che" Guevara was born in Rosario, Argentina, and studied medicine in Buenos Aires. Forced to leave Argentina for political reasons in 1952, he met the Cuban rebel leader Fidel Castro in Mexico, and joined his invasion of Cuba in 1956. By 1959 the rebels had taken control of the island. Guevara was put in charge of the Cuban National Bank, but his real interest lay in promoting revolution. He left Cuba in 1965 and was eventually killed while trying to stimulate a peasant uprising in Bolivia.

EL DIARIO DEL **CHE** EN BOLIVIA noviembre 7, 1966 a octubre 7, 1967

Youth hero
Guevara's death at the hands of Bolivian soldiers in October 1967 only enhanced his status as a folk hero with young people around the world. Posters of "Che" adorned the walls of students' rooms, alongside pictures of the Beatles or other pop idols. Some of his appeal was undoubtedly due to his good looks, but his taste for revolutionary violence also attracted 1960s students, many of whom were committed to the pursuit of radical social change.

Propaganda posters frequently used Guevara's image.

Nadine Gordimer
b. 1923

South African author Nadine Gordimer grew up in a white, middle-class family outside Johannesburg. Her writing depicts the narrow, restricted lives of white South Africans, and attacks the racial segregation that protects their comfortable lifestyles. She published her first short story collection, *Face to Face*, in 1949. Her recurring theme is seen clearly in her first novel, *The Lying Days* (1953), about a girl's fight against her parents' racism. Her best-known book is *The Conservationist* (1974), which contrasts the world of white South Africa with the myths and rituals of the Zulus. Gordimer's sharp observation of a country that has had the eyes of the world upon it has given her an international readership. In 1991 she was awarded the Nobel Prize for literature. Since the end of apartheid, she has continued to subject South African society to balanced and critical scrutiny.

KEY PUBLICATIONS

1952	*The Soft Voice of the Serpent* (short stories)
1953	*The Lying Days* (novel)
1965	*Not For Publication* (short stories)
1971	*Livingstone's Companions* (short stories)
1974	*The Conservationist* (novel)
1979	*Burger's Daughter* (novel)
1981	*July's People* (novel)
1987	*A Sport of Nature* (novel)
1994	*None to Accompany Me* (novel)

Vaclav Havel
b. 1936

The Czech writer and statesman Vaclav Havel started out as a stagehand at a Prague theatre. In 1960, he became resident writer there. His most famous early play was *The Garden Party* (1963). Havel was a prominent figure in the 1968 "Prague Spring", a drive to liberalize Czechoslovakia's communist regime. After the Soviet Union and its allies invaded the country later that year, his plays were banned and his passport was seized. During the 1970s and 1980s he was arrested several times and spent four years in prison for his attempts to improve human rights in Czechoslovakia. He was one of the founders of Charter '77 – a group dedicated to freedom of expression – and circulated the work of banned writers. He also continued to write plays. After communist rule collapsed in 1989, Havel was elected president of Czechoslovakia. In 1992, he resigned in protest at the breakaway of Slovakia, but he returned as president of the new Czech Republic in 1993.

Anti-communist demonstration in Prague

Velvet Revolution

In November 1989, mass demonstrations were held in Prague, the capital of Czechoslovakia, calling for an end to communist rule. On 24 November, the communist government yielded to popular pressure and resigned. Vaclav Havel was elected as the country's president at the end of December. The almost bloodless collapse of communism in Czechoslovakia is often referred to as the "Velvet Revolution".

Bob Hawke
b. 1929

Bob Hawke, one of Australia's most striking political personalities, was born in Bordertown, South Australia. He studied economics at the University of Western Australia and at Oxford University, England. Hawke was a member of the Australian Labor Party from 1946 and, after university, became prominent in the trade union movement, rising to president of the Australian Council of Trade Unions in 1969. In 1980 he was elected to the Federal Parliament and soon challenged Bill Hayden for leadership of the Labor party. In 1983, Liberal prime minister Malcolm Fraser called a snap election, hoping to take advantage of dissent in the Labor leadership, but Hayden stood down and Hawke led Labor to election victory. He was prime minister for the next eight years, winning three more elections. Hawke prided himself on his skills as a conciliator, but was always an outspoken figure. In 1991, he was ousted as prime minister by a member of his own cabinet, Paul Keating.

Stephen Hawking
b. 1942

British physicist Stephen Hawking studied physics at Oxford University and went on to take a doctorate at Cambridge, where he was made a research fellow. Shortly afterwards, he contracted a neuromuscular disease which is incurable and gets progressively worse with time. In spite of his deteriorating physical condition, he established himself as one of the world's foremost cosmologists, using mathematics and theoretical physics to explore the nature and origins of the universe. He showed that Einstein's theory of relativity implied the universe must have begun with a Big Bang and was destined to end in black holes, collapsed stars from which neither light nor anything else can ever escape. Paradoxically, one of Hawking's greatest achievements was to show that no black hole could be completely black – they all emit radiation and eventually disappear. This is known as the Hawking Process. Since 1979, Hawking has been Lucasian Professor of Mathematics at Cambridge, a position once held by the great 17th-century physicist Isaac Newton. Hawking's book *A Brief History of Time*, published in 1988, is one of the century's most unlikely bestsellers. Its lucid explanation of the difficult theories of modern physics made Hawking known to a broad international public.

Hawking communicates using a computerised "voice".

Sir Alfred Hitchcock
1899–1989

London-born film director Alfred Hitchcock first entered the movie industry as a commercial artist designing credits. He directed his first movies in the mid-1920s, but only became prominent a decade later with the success of the thriller *The 39 Steps*. He moved from England to Hollywood in 1940 and his first American film, *Rebecca*, won an Oscar for best picture. He confirmed his reputation as the "master of suspense" with a series of memorable movie dramas, including *Notorious* and *Strangers on a Train* (1951). Now highly regarded, *Rear Window* (1954) and *Vertigo* (1958) were not a great success when first released, but a turn towards horror brought the director to the peak of his career in the early 1960s, with the shockers *Psycho* and *The Birds*. Hitchcock was better known to the general public than any other film director. He always appeared as an extra in his own movies, and he also hosted two successful television series.

Poster for *The Birds*, 1963

Cheng Ho
1371–1433

Cheng Ho, also known as Zheng He, was born into a Muslim family in Ming China. He became a eunuch at the imperial court and a close adviser to Emperor Ming Yongle. In 1405, the emperor entrusted him with command of a fleet of ocean-going junks that were to sail around Southeast Asia and across the Indian Ocean. The aim of the voyage was to assert China's authority over this vast area and to support Chinese traders. Cheng Ho's fleet was huge, comprising more than 60 large junks, over 200 support vessels, and almost 30,000 men. It travelled as far as the east coast of Africa and brought back exotic rareties, such as a giraffe for the emperor's zoo. Cheng Ho made a total of seven such voyages between 1405 and 1433, before the Chinese imperial government decided to turn its back on the outside world and abandoned any further marine exploration.

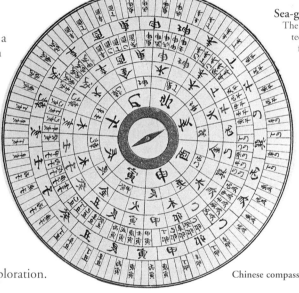
Chinese compass

Sea-going technology
The Chinese were advanced in all the technology and techniques required for oceanic exploration. In particular, the Chinese had a marine compass from around 1000 AD. The invention was later adopted by European sailors. Chinese ocean-going junks were formidable vessels with a powerful armament and a large crew. China's sudden abandonment of ocean voyages in the 1430s, however, meant that in the 1500s European ships began sailing to Chinese ports, rather than Chinese vessels reaching European ports, as could so easily have been the case.

Grace Hopper
1906–92

American computer scientist Grace Hopper was educated at Vassar College and Yale. During World War II, she volunteered for duty with the Naval Office Computation Project. In 1945, she was sent to Harvard University to assist Howard Aiken in the building of a computer. Her main contribution was to create the first computer language, together with the compiler necessary to translate it into a form that the computer could work with. In 1959, she joined a US Defense Department team trying to create a simple computer language for commercial use. This led to the invention of COBOL (Common Business-Oriented Language), still one of the most widely used computer languages.

King Hussein
1935–99

The British-educated Jordanian monarch ibn Talal Hussein came to the throne in 1953. He was favourably disposed to the West, but the growing pressure of Arab nationalism forced him to adopt a difficult balancing act between the two sides. Hussein relied on the Jordanian army to maintain power against the demands of an expanding Palestinian population that had no traditional loyalty to his dynasty. His involvement on the Arab side during the 1967 Arab-Israeli war led to a massive influx of Palestinian refugees, whose support for the PLO dangerously destabilized Hussein's kingdom. In 1971, however, Hussein expelled the PLO from Jordan. Although he backed Saddam Hussein during the 1991 Gulf conflict, Hussein advocated peace between Israel and the Arab states. He relinquished his rights to the West Bank and played an important negotiating role in the 1999 peace agreement before his death from cancer.

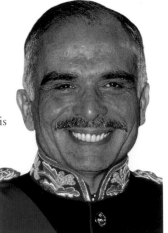

KEY REIGN DATES

1956 Political unrest forces Hussein to sever links with the West and dismiss Western military advisors.

1967 Suffers a severe military defeat during the Arab-Israeli war, losing the West Bank to Israel.

1970 Calls in the army to suppress PLO guerrilla activity in Jordan.

1988 Surrenders claim to the West Bank and cedes right of representing Palestinians there to the PLO.

1991 Temporarily loses Western aid as a result of support for Saddam Hussein during Gulf conflict.

1999 Orders his brother, Crown Prince Hassan, to step down in favour of his eldest son, Prince Abdullah.

Mohammed Ali Jinnah
1876–1948

Mohammed Ali Jinnah was born into an Indian Muslim family during the period of British rule in India. After studying law in London he qualified as a lawyer in 1897, and subsequently set up a successful law practice in Bombay. Entering politics in 1906, Jinnah campaigned for independence from Britain, and became president of the Muslim League in 1916. Initially, he supported the aims of the Hindu-dominated National Congress Party, attending the Round Table Conference of 1930–31 and working with Congress leaders during negotiations before and after the setting up of the 1935 constitution. During the late 1930s, however, he gradually became convinced that Hindus and Muslims could not live together harmoniously and that the Muslims must have their own homeland. The Congress Party was against any division of the sub-continent, but Jinnah was adamant and through skillful negotiation convinced the British to accept partition. Despite vociferous and, at times, violent opposition from the Hindu majority, Mohammed Ali Jinnah achieved his aim in 1947 when, following British withdrawal, he became the first governor-general of the new Muslim state of Pakistan.

Michael Jordan
b. 1963

Born in Brooklyn, New York, the basketball star Michael Jordan acquired his reputation as a superbly talented player while at college, taking the University of North Carolina to victory in the national collegiate championships. Jordan joined the Chicago Bulls as a professional player in 1985, where he earned the nickname "Air Jordan" because of his sheer athleticism and ability to outjump opponents. As well as helping the team to victory in six National Basketball Association (NBA) finals, Jordan was the first basketball player to be named Most Valuable Player (MVP) five times by the NBA. One of the highest scorers in the game, Jordan made more than 50 points on 34 different occasions, holding the record for the most points (63) scored in a National Basketball Association play-off (against Boston in 1986). Jordan suddenly announced his retirement in 1993, much to the surprise and disappointment of his many fans, and began a new career as a minor league baseball player. The lure of basketball proved too great, however, and Jordan rejoined the Chicago Bulls in 1995. Jordan was arguably the most exciting – and certainly the best paid – basketball player of the 1980s and 1990s.

KEY CAREER DATES

1982 Leads University of North Carolina to a National Collegiate Athletic Association championship.

1984 Plays for the US national basketball team at the Los Angeles Olympics and wins a gold medal.

1992 Wins a further gold medal with the famed "Dream Team" at the Barcelona Olympics.

1994 Declared to be the world's top paid sportsman with an annual income in excess of $30 million.

1998 Leading the Chicago Bulls, wins the NBA championship in a close 87-86 victory over the Utah Jazz.

Thomas Keneally
b. 1935

Australian novelist Thomas Keneally was born in New South Wales and underwent training to become a Roman Catholic priest. Before ordination, however, he left to become a teacher and then a full-time writer. Many of Keneally's books have historical themes, and include *Gossip from the Forest* (1975), which focuses on the Armistice negotiations of 1918, and the American Civil War epic *Confederates* (1979). His 1968 novel, *Three Cheers for the Paraclete*, established his reputation as a writer of promise, although it was the Booker prize-winning novel *Schindler's Ark* (1982) which brought him to an international audience. Keneally is also a prominent supporter of the republican movement in Australia, and expressed his passionately held views in *Our Republic* (1993).

Books into films, words into gold
In addition to reaping the rewards of having an international readership, Keneally has profited from having several of his books adapted for the big screen. The most famous adaptation of a Keneally novel was Steven Spielberg's 1993 reworking of *Schindler's Ark*, which was both an artistic and commercial success. Re-titled *Schindler's List*, it told the story of a German industrialist saving the lives of the Jews who worked in his factories.

John F. Kennedy
1917–63

The 35th president of the United States, John Fitzgerald Kennedy was born into a politically active Roman Catholic family of Irish descent. Graduating from Harvard in 1940, he served with distinction during World War II and was decorated for gallantry after rescuing crew members of his sunken patrol boat after it had been rammed. Following the war, Kennedy entered politics, and as a member of the Democratic party he served first as a congressman and then as a senator for Massachusetts. He defeated the Republican Richard Nixon in the 1960 elections to become, at the age of 43, the youngest ever American president. Kennedy's reforming social measures were blocked for the most part by a hostile Congress, although his support for the civil rights movement had lasting influence. His handling of foreign affairs, however, gave him more scope to exercise his forceful idealism.

After the fiasco of the Bay of Pigs episode in 1961 (a US-backed attempt by Cuban exiles to invade Cuba), Kennedy won international acclaim for his calm and resolute management of the 1962 Cuban Missile Crisis. Refusing to be browbeaten by Soviet leader Nikita Khrushchev, Kennedy forced the Russians to dismantle the missile bases they had built on the island. He also confronted the Soviet Union over the security of Berlin and stepped up US involvement in Indochina. Kennedy pledged to Congress that the United States would land a man on the Moon ahead of the Soviet Union and by the end of the decade – a pledge that was to prove correct. A youthful and dynamic figure – ably supported by his photogenic wife Jackie – Kennedy set the tone for a new, youthful style of presidency, which proved popular around the world. But Kennedy's term of office came to an abrupt and tragic end when he was shot and killed during an official visit to Dallas, Texas.

Style and substance
In 1953 Kennedy married the beautiful and sophisticated Jacqueline Bouvier. She played an important role in promoting his political career, providing an aura of glamour that had previously been lacking in US political life. Despite the fact that Kennedy was a well-known philanderer, Jackie remained loyal to her husband and was by his side when he was shot in Dallas. She married Greek shipping tycoon Aristotle Onassis in 1968, and after his death in 1975 she returned to the US, pursuing a career as a book editor until her death from cancer in 1994.

KEY CAREER DATES

1912 Begins working as a nurse in the bush country of Australia.

1915 Accepted into the Australian army nursing corps, where she remains until 1919.

1933 Sets up a clinic in Australia which acts as a showcase for her pioneering work in the treatment of the poliomyelitis disease.

1943 Publishes her autobiography entitled *And They Shall Walk*, which describes her career as nurse and medical pioneer.

Elizabeth Kenny
1886–1952

The Australian nurse Elizabeth Kenny began her career working as a bush nurse. During World War I she joined the Australian army nursing corps, where she gained wide experience of battlefield injuries. But Kenny's major contribution in the field of nursing came in the inter-war period when she developed new techniques for treating patients with poliomyelitis. Instead of using the traditional method of immobilizing the polio sufferer with casts and splints, she pioneered the use of muscle therapy, which in many cases produced better results. Kenny travelled widely to demonstrate her methods of treatment, and established clinics in Australia, Britain, and the United States. Known to her patients as "Sister Kenny", she did much to raise the profile of nursing.

Genghis Khan
1162–1227

Originally called Temujin, the Mongol leader Genghis Khan was born in Mongolia in central Asia, the son of a local chief. He succeeded his father at the age of 13 and slowly built up Mongol power in the region. In 1206 a *kuriltai*, an assembly of all the Mongol tribes, proclaimed him Genghis Khan ("Universal Ruler"). Over the next 15 years, his armies swept all before them, conquering northern China, Afghanistan, central Asia, and much of Persia, creating an empire that stretched from the China Sea in the east to the Black Sea in the west. Genghis Khan was not only a fearsome warrior but a sound administrator who welded the warring Mongolian tribes into a superb fighting machine.

Ayatollah Khomeini
1902–89

Born Sayyed Ruhollah in the Iranian town of Khomein (from which he took his name), Khomeini grew up to become a leading Islamic scholar and teacher (ayatollah). Actively opposing the Westernizing policies of the Shah of Iran, he was expelled from the country in 1964, spending his exile in Iraq and France. During this period Khomeini became the acknowledged leader of the Iranian opposition, and he returned in triumph to Iran after the overthrow of the Shah in 1979. Khomeini was installed as the leader of a new religious government that reversed the course of modernization and crushed all internal dissent. His virulent anti-Western policies soon brought him into conflict with the United States. He sanctioned the storming of the US Embassy in Tehran in 1979, and his government played a major role in the sponsorship of international terrorism. Although some attempts were made to normalize relations with the West, shortly before his death he called for the murder of the British writer Salman Rushdie whom, he claimed, had insulted the Islamic religion.

Religious revolution
The increasing social inequalities experienced in Iran in the late 1970s led to popular protest against the Western "decadence" of the ruling elites. As other potential opposition groups had been ruthlessly suppressed by the Iranian secret police, the focus of opposition was centred around the religious ayatollahs, who had always condemned the Shah's modernizing policies. Mass protests brought the country to a virtual standstill by 1979, forcing the Shah to abdicate. The ensuing collapse of the government produced a power vacuum in Iran, which left the way clear for the ayatollahs to take over and impose their own religious rule.

F.W. de Klerk
b. 1936

South African politician F.W. de Klerk was born in Johannesburg, and in 1972 was elected to the South African Parliament as a National Party member. He served in the cabinet of P.W. Botha from 1978 onwards, and when Botha fell ill in 1989, de Klerk took over as leader of the National Party and acting state president. Once in power he began to dismantle the apartheid system. In 1990 he lifted the 30-year-old ban on the black opposition movement, the African National Congress (ANC), and agreed to the release of its leader Nelson Mandela (the two men were jointly awarded the Nobel Peace Prize in 1993). In 1994 South Africa held its first all-race national elections, which were won by the ANC. While Mandela became president, de Klerk accepted the post of vice-president. In 1996, however, de Klerk resigned his post, taking the National Party into opposition.

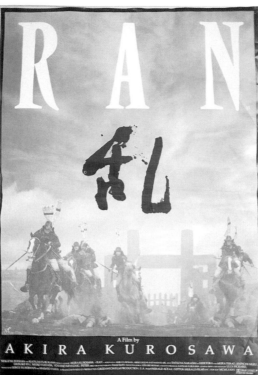

KEY KUROSAWA FILMS

1951 *The Idiot* (based on Dostoievski's novel of the same name)

1957 *Throne of Blood* (based on Shakespeare's play *Macbeth*)

1957 *Donzoko* (an adaptation of Gorky's novel *The Lower Depths*)

1975 *Dersu Uzala* (the story of a Siberian hunter)

1985 *Ran* (a reworking of Shakespeare's play *King Lear*)

1980 *Kagemusha* (an epic tale of clan warfare among Japan's samurai)

Akira Kurosawa
1910–98

The Japanese film director Akira Kurosawa was born in Tokyo and first studied as a painter, a training that was reflected in his skill in composition and in the exquisite use of colour in his later films. After working for several years as a film editor and screenwriter he made his directorial debut with *Sanshiro Sugato* in 1943. Two major influences on his filmmaking were traditional Japanese Noh theatre and the classics of Western literature. His first international success was *Rashomon* (1950), a complex multi-layered story set in medieval Japan which won the Venice Film Festival Prize. *Seven Samurai* (1954) was another medieval story that proved highly influential in the West. Kurosawa continued to produce films of the highest quality throughout his life, and can be regarded as one of the great directors in the history of cinema.

Dalai Lama
b. 1935

The spiritual leader of Tibet, the 14th Dalai Lama (originally Tenzin Gyatso) was born into a peasant family in Taktser, in Amdo Province. At the age of two the monks of Lhasa identified him as the reincarnation of the Compassionate Buddha. He was taken from his parents, trained as a Buddhist monk, and enthroned in 1940, but did not assume power until 10 years later. Following the 1950 uprising against the Chinese, who had occupied Tibet, the Dalai Lama negotiated a settlement with the Chinese and acted as nominal ruler of the kingdom. However, Chinese rule grew increasingly harsh and in 1959 the Tibetans staged another uprising which the Chinese suppressed. The Dalai Lama fled into exile in India, setting up an alternative Tibetan government. Since then he has devoted his life to campaigning for the independence of Tibet. A highly revered figure, he has gained great international sympathy for his people's plight, and includes film stars and other celebrities among his supporters. But as yet he has been unable to convince the Chinese government to relax its hold over Tibet. In 1989 he was awarded the Nobel Peace Prize in recognition of his non-violent opposition to Chinese rule.

Spike Lee
b. 1957

The American film director and actor Spike (Shelton Jackson) Lee grew up in New York, the son of a jazz musician. From an early age Lee showed an interest in films, and made amateur movies while in high school. Lee studied film at New York University's Institute of Film and Television, where he won a student academy award for his film *Joe's Bed-Stuy Barbershop: We Cut Heads*. After graduation he sunk his talent and assets into the low-budget movie, *She's Gotta Have It*, which provided him with a reputation as a director of great promise. A filmmaker prepared to make controversial films and equally controversial public statements, he has repeatedly attacked racism in American society. He acts in many of his own films and has also directed a large number of music videos. As part of his commitment to combat racism, Spike Lee helped the African-American politician Jesse Jackson during the 1988 presidential election campaign.

SPIKE LEE MOVIES	
1980	*The Answer* (student film)
1981	*Sarah* (student film)
1982	*Joe's Bed-Stuy Barbershop: We Cut Heads* (student film)
1986	*She's Gotta Have It* (an amusing comedy that proved an immediate critical and commercial success)
1988	*School Daze*
1989	*Do the Right Thing* (an acerbic comedy on the role of African-Americans in the United States)
1990	*Mo Better Blues*
1991	*Jungle Fever*
1992	*Malcolm X* (a powerful biography of the murdered African-American civil rights leader)
1994	*Crooklyn*
1995	*Clockers*
1996	*Girl 6*
1996	*Get on the Bus*
1997	*4 Little Girls*
1998	*He Got Game*
1999	*Summer of Sam*

C.S. Lewis
1898–1963

The British academic and writer Clive Staples Lewis was born in Belfast, Northern Ireland, the son of a solicitor. After being wounded in World War I, Lewis went to Oxford University – as scholar, fellow, and tutor – until moving to Cambridge to become Professor of Medieval and Renaissance English in 1954. A writer with an extensive range of styles and subject matter, he published *The Allegory of Love* (1936), a treatise on medieval courtly love, and a number of books on Christian belief, of which *The Screwtape Letters* (1942) became a best-seller. Lewis also wrote several works of science fiction, although he is probably best known for his children's books, which include the *Chronicles of Narnia* series.

Lewis photographed in 1950

Charles Lindbergh
1902–74

The American aviator Charles Lindbergh was born in Detroit, Michigan, and after gaining his pilot's licence in 1925 worked as one of the early air-mail pilots on the Chicago–St. Louis run. In 1927 he made the world's first solo non-stop transatlantic flight, taking off from New York in his monoplane *Spirit of St. Louis* and landing 33 hours later at an airfield near Paris. He became an international celebrity, and undertook further long-distance flights, many with his wife. In 1932 their infant son was kidnapped and murdered, a sensational crime that shocked American society and which led to the execution of Bruno Hauptman four years later. Impressed by the strength of the German air force, Lindbergh campaigned for America's neutrality during World War II. In 1953 he published his autobiography *The Spirit of St. Louis*, which was awarded the Pulitzer Prize.

Ding Ling
1904–86

Radical feminist, novelist, and short-story writer, Ding Ling – pseudonym of Jiang Bingzhi – was born in the Hunan province of China. Moving to Beijing, she enrolled in the university and was greatly influenced by the growing communist movement in China. In 1928 she published *The Diary of Miss Sophia*, which approached the subjects of female psychology and sexual desire with unusual frankness. As a member of the Communist Party she was briefly imprisoned before escaping to the communist stronghold of Yenan in 1936. Her outspoken views on the role of women in society earned her the displeasure of the party leadership, until her land-reform novel *The Sun Shines over the Sanggan River* (1948) brought her back into favour. In 1958, however, she again fell foul of the system and was banished to the Great Northern Wilderness. In 1970 she was imprisoned for five years as a consequence of the turmoil caused by the Chinese Cultural Revolution. In 1979 Ding Ling was at last rehabilitated on a permanent basis by the Communist Party, and published a novel based on her experiences of exile, *Comrade Du Wanxing*.

Thomas Malthus
1766–1834

The English economist and pioneer of demography studied at Cambridge before entering the Church of England as a clergyman. In his famous publication *An Essay on the Principle of Population* (published anonymously in 1798 and subsequently revised in 1807), Malthus advanced the argument that populations – both animal and human – tend to increase faster than their means of subsistence. This tendency towards over-population was slowed by the actions of war, famine and disease, although, he reasoned, humans could take a more positive intervention through "moral restraint" (celibacy) or birth control. His pessimistic views contrasted markedly with contemporary beliefs in the perfectibility of man, and he was attacked by radicals and conservatives alike. Although he failed to comprehend the potential of industrial and agricultural improvement to offset the consequences of an expanding population, Malthus was the first thinker to address the problem of population growth, a matter of serious concern in our own century.

KEY CAREER DATES

1793 Becomes a Fellow of Jesus College, Cambridge, distinguishing himself in mathematics.

1797 Appointed curate of the parish of Albury in Surrey.

1798 Publishes his *Essay on the Principle of Population*.

1805 Appointed professor of political economy at Haileybury College.

1820 Publishes *Principles of Political Economy*, an influential economic treatise anticipating the work of economist David Ricardo.

Katherine Mansfield
1888–1923

The writer Kathleen Mansfield Beauchamp was born in Wellington, New Zealand, and educated in New Zealand and England. In 1908 she arrived in London determined to pursue a career as a writer, living a bohemian life that saw her meet, marry and leave her first husband George Bowden in the space of three weeks. In 1911 Mansfield discovered she was pregnant (not by her husband) and was sent to a hotel in Bavaria, where she suffered a miscarriage. This experience was to become the basis of her first collection of stories, *In a German Pension*. Later in 1911 she met and lived with the editor and critic John Middleton Murry. She married him after her divorce in 1918. Mansfield became a leading member of the London literary scene, mixing with other writers of the day, most notably D.H. Lawrence, who portrayed her as Gudrun in his novel *Women in Love*. She produced several collections of short stories, which displayed an innovative, sensitive, yet often ironic style, and confirmed her mastery of this literary form. In 1916 she and Murry founded the magazine *Signature*, but the onset of tuberculosis forced her to increasingly limit her activities to writing. She subsequently died of the disease in France. Mansfield's stormy relationship with Murry – which involved lengthy separations – was revealed in the posthumous publication of her *Letters to John Middleton Murry* (1951).

MANSFIELD'S WORKS

1911 *In a German Pension*

1917 *Prelude* (her first major work, which explored her childhood experiences in New Zealand)

1920 *Bliss, and Other Stories* (a mature work that established her fame)

1922 *The Garden Party* (containing some of her best known stories, including "The Daughters of the Late Colonel" and "The Voyage")

1924 *Something Childish* (a posthumous collection of stories)

Golda Meir
1898–1978

Golda Meir was born Goldie Mabovitch in Kiev, Ukraine. When she was eight years old, her Jewish family emigrated to the United States, settling in Milwaukee, Wisconsin. She married in 1917 and moved to Palestine, then under British control, four years later, living on a kibbutz and becoming active in the Jewish labour movement. After World War II, she was a leading figure in the struggle for an independent Israel, and signed the declaration of independence in 1948. After holding a series of diplomatic and government posts, Meir was elected Israeli prime minister in 1969. She strove to make peace between the Arabs and Israelis, but her efforts failed when war broke out in 1973. She resigned the following year. When she died, it was revealed that she had been suffering from leukemia for 12 years.

KEY CAREER DATES

1928 Becomes executive secretary of the Jewish Women's Labour Council.

1936 Named head of the political department of the General Federation of Jewish Labour.

1948 Appointed Israeli ambassador to the Soviet Union.

1949 Becomes minister of labour in the Israeli government.

1956 Becomes Israeli foreign minister, a post she holds for 10 years.

1966 Elected secretary-general of the Israeli Labour Party.

1969 Becomes prime minister.

1973 Leads Israel through the Yom Kippur War.

1974 Resigns as prime minister after criticism of alleged unpreparedness for the Yom Kippur War.

KEY MONROE FILMS

1953 *Gentlemen Prefer Blondes*, with Jane Russell, directed by Howard Hawkes

1955 *The Seven Year Itch*, directed by Billy Wilder

1957 *The Prince and the Showgirl*, with Sir Laurence Olivier

1959 *Some Like It Hot*, directed by Billy Wilder

1961 *The Misfits*, with Clark Gable, directed by John Huston

Monroe with her third husband, Arthur Miller

Marilyn Monroe
1926–62

American film star Marilyn Monroe was born Norma Jean Mortenson in Los Angeles, California. She spent her childhood in orphanages and a series of foster homes. After a spell as a photographer's model and minor Hollywood starlet, she made her breakthrough as the latest screen "sex goddess" in 1953. Her brief marriage to baseball star Joe DiMaggio the following year further raised her public profile. Although dismissed initially as a "dumb blonde", Monroe soon revealed genuine acting talent in comedies such as *The Seven Year Itch* and *Some Like it Hot*. She continued, however, to aspire to be taken more seriously. In 1956 she married the intellectual playwright Arthur Miller, and he wrote the script for her last film, *The Misfits*. Monroe divorced Miller at the beginning of 1961, by which time she was suffering severe depression. Because of her increasingly erratic behaviour, she was sacked by her film studio, 20th Century Fox, in July 1962. She died a month later from an overdose of sleeping pills. Her rags-to-riches life and early death – she was only 36 years old – have come to symbolize the glamour and tragedy of stardom.

Toni Morrison
b. 1931

African-American writer Toni Morrison was born Chloe Anthony Wofford in Lorain, Ohio. She grew up in the Midwest, before attending Howard University in Washington, D.C., and Cornell University, New York. Morrison taught writing at Howard and then edited fiction for a New York publishing house. She wrote her first novel, *The Bluest Eye*, in 1969. *Sula* followed in 1973, but it was *Song of Solomon* in 1977 that shot Morrison to fame. In 1987, *Beloved* won the Pulitzer Prize for fiction. Morrison was awarded the Nobel Prize for literature in 1993, an honour that confirmed her standing as one of the world's leading novelists. Her novels deal with the African-American story – an often violent tale of struggle and injustice, which Morrison tells in a style that is poetic, yet brutally cold-blooded. *Paradise*, her first novel since winning the Nobel Prize, appeared in 1997.

Guru Nanak
1469–1539

Guru ("teacher") Nanak was the founder of the Sikh religion. He was born in a village near Lahore, in what is now Pakistan. Brought up as a Hindu, Nanak also studied Islam and had Muslim friends. According to Sikh tradition, he had a vision one day while bathing in a stream. He came out of the stream saying, "there is no Hindu, there is no Muslim", and went on to found a new religion to bring together the two older faiths. He rejected the Hindu caste system, which put people in different ranks, with "untouchables" at the bottom – Nanak said that everyone was equal before God. His followers were called Sikhs, which means "disciples". Today there are almost 20 million Sikhs, most living in the Punjab in northwest India.

Admiral Horatio Nelson
1758–1805

Lady Emma Hamilton

NELSON'S KEY BATTLES

1797 With Sir John Jervis, defeats the Spanish fleet off Cape St. Vincent.

1798 Destroys the French fleet off Aboukir Bay, Egypt, in the Battle of the Nile.

1801 Sinks the neutral Danish fleet at the Battle of Copenhagen, ignoring orders to disengage.

1805 Defeats the combined French and Spanish fleets at the Battle of Trafalgar, but dies on board *Victory*.

The most famous commander in British naval history, Horatio Nelson was born in Burnham Thorpe, Norfolk. He first went to sea as a midshipman at the age of 12, and by the time he was 17 he had already sailed to the West Indies, the Arctic, and the Indian Ocean. He took part in Britain's sea war against the American colonists and their French allies during the American War of Independence, before marrying Fanny Nisbet and retiring to his birthplace in 1787. Recalled to service to fight the French in 1793, he lost his left eye in the siege of Calvi, Corsica. In 1797, he also lost his right arm, amputated after he was hit by grapeshot at Santa Cruz in the Canary Islands. Undeterred, the following year Nelson inflicted a devastating defeat on the French fleet supporting Napoleon's expedition to Egypt. The Battle of the Nile made him a national hero. It also won him the admiration of the wife of the British ambassador in Naples, Lady Emma Hamilton. After playing a part in the brutal suppression of a revolution against the king of Naples, Nelson went back to England with Lady Hamilton, by whom he had a daughter. In 1803, he returned to the Mediterranean as commander of the British fleet, and in October 1805 he engaged the French and Spanish fleets off Cape Trafalgar, Spain, crushing them and bringing an end to French naval power for the remainder of the Napoleonic Wars. However, Nelson himself was shot during the battle, and died at sea. He was given a national hero's funeral, but the British government refused his last request for them to support Lady Hamilton and his daughter.

Pablo Neruda
1904–73

Chilean poet Neftalí Ricardo Reyes began to write poetry at the age of 10. Under the pen name Pablo Neruda, he had great popular success in the 1920s, especially with his book *Twenty Love Poems and a Song of Despair*. Needing a steady income, he embarked on a career as a diplomat in 1927. By the time he returned to Chile in 1943, he had become a communist. He was exiled for his political views from 1946 to 1952, but his reputation as a poet continued to grow. He was awarded the Nobel Prize for literature in 1971.

MAJOR POETRY

1923 *Crepusculario*

1924 *Veinte poemas de amor y una canción desesperada (Twenty Love Poems and a Song of Despair)*

1925–31 *Residencia en la Tierra (Residence on Earth, two volumes)*

1945 *Alturas de Macchu Picchu (The Heights of Macchu Picchu)*

1950 *Canto General*

1954 *Odas elementales (The Elementary Odes)*

1969 *Fin de mundo (The End of the World)*

Rudolf Nureyev
1938–93

Born in Irkutsk, Siberia, the Russian ballet dancer Rudolf Nureyev trained at the Kirov School in Leningrad (now St. Petersburg) and became a principal dancer for the Kirov Ballet. In 1961, he defected from the Soviet Union while on a visit to Paris. A year later he began a partnership with the British ballerina Margot Fonteyn at the Royal Ballet in London, dancing the principal roles in ballets such as *Swan Lake* and *Giselle*. Together, Fonteyn and Nureyev helped to bring ballet to a wider audience. Nureyev was able to express intense emotion through his body, and is credited with having re-established the importance of the role of the male dancer. He was artistic director of the Paris Opera Ballet from 1983 to 1989.

Sir Laurence Olivier
1907–89

British actor and director Laurence Olivier was born in Surrey, England, and studied at the Central School of Dramatic Art in London. His early career on stage and screen was undistinguished, but in 1937 he made his name with a memorable performance as Hamlet for the Old Vic Company. By the end of the decade he had also established himself as a Hollywood star, marrying the actress Vivien Leigh, his second wife, in 1940. Olivier was soon being hailed as the finest Shakespearian actor of his generation – he played Hamlet, Henry V, Richard lll, and Othello both on stage and in films that he directed himself. He grew to be a highly influential figure in British theatre and, in 1947, became the first actor to receive a knighthood. In 1961, he married his third wife, actress Joan Plowright. The following year, he was appointed director of the new National Theatre in London, a post he held until 1973. In his later years, he appeared only in films and on television.

KEY MOVIE ROLES

1939	Heathcliff in *Wuthering Heights*
1940	Maxim de Winter in *Rebecca*
1944	Title role, *Henry V*, also director
1948	Title role, *Hamlet*, also director
1955	Title role, *Richard III*, also director
1960	Archie Rice in *The Entertainer*

George Orwell
1903–50

English writer Eric Arthur Blair, better known by his pen name, George Orwell, was born in Bengal, India, the son of a British official in the Indian civil service. Educated on a scholarship at Eton, Orwell refused to go to university, instead joining the Indian Civil Police in Burma. In 1927, ashamed of British colonialism, he returned to Europe to become a writer. Orwell spent time in slums and with the homeless, experiences reflected in his books *Down and Out in Paris and London* (1933) and *The Road to Wigan Pier* (1937). He also fought on the Republican side in the Spanish Civil War, an adventure recounted in *Homage to Catalonia* (1938). His last book, *1984*, was published in 1949.

Cartoon version of *Animal Farm*

Satirical vision
Orwell was a socialist, but a bitter opponent of Soviet-style communism. In 1945, he wrote *Animal Farm*, the story of a revolution that ends up creating a society as bad as the one it replaced. His last book, *1984*, describes a terrifying world in which the dictator Big Brother watches over every citizen, and torture is used to ensure total conformism.

Pelé
b. 1940

Brazilian footballer Edson Arantes do Nascimento has always been known simply as Pelé. He earned this nickname at an early age from his skill at *pedala*, a simple version of football, which he played in the streets as a child. Pelé made his international debut in 1957, at the age of 16. He won his first World Cup medal the following year, scoring two goals in Brazil's 4-2 victory over Sweden in the final. In the 1962 and 1966 World Cups he was frustrated by injury, but his fine performance in Brazil's cup-winning side in Mexico in 1970 crowned his career. Pelé officially retired from football in 1974, but returned to play for the New York Cosmos in the North American Soccer League from 1975 to 1977. He has since devoted himself to encouraging the Brazilian footballers of the future.

CAREER HIGHLIGHTS

1956 Plays his first game for Brazilian club Santos.

1957 Plays his first match for Brazil, against Argentina.

1958 Helps Brazil win the World Cup in Sweden.

1964 Scores eight goals in one game for Santos.

1969 Scores his 1,000th goal in professional football.

1970 Stars in Brazil's 4-1 World Cup final win over Italy.

Samuel Pepys
1623–1703

English diarist Samuel Pepys was born in London, England. He came from a humble background, but rose to be a principal officer of the Navy Board from 1660, and secretary to the Admiralty from 1673 to 1688. This role as a naval administrator remained his only claim to a place in history until 1825, when his diaries, written in code, were first deciphered. Begun in 1660, they provide a fascinating, detailed account of life in London in the Restoration period. Pepys describes major historical events such as the Plague of 1665 and the Great Fire of London, but his diary is also an exceptionally frank record of his private life. Pepys gave up keeping a diary in 1669 because of failing eyesight.

Eva Peron
1919–52

Eva Peron, known as "Evita", was born Maria Eva Duarte, the fifth child of a poor family in Buenos Aires, Argentina. She was a minor actress when she married Colonel Juan Domingo Peron in December 1945. He was a politically ambitious army officer who had been secretary of labour and welfare in the Argentinian government, a position he had used to build up support among the country's workers and poor – the *descamisados,* or "shirtless ones". In 1946, he was elected president of Argentina. As first lady, Evita organized the women's branch of the Peronista party. She also created the Eva Peron Foundation, designed to provide housing, clothing, and money for the poor. She was an immensely popular figure in Argentina, but her ambition to become vice-president was blocked by the opposition of conservative military officers. Evita died of cancer in July 1952. Her life story was used as the basis for a hit musical, *Evita*, in 1978.

Marcel Proust
1871–1922

French novelist Marcel Proust was born at Auteuil in the Paris suburbs, the son of a doctor. From his childhood onwards he suffered from chronic asthma, but despite his sickly disposition he studied law at the Sorbonne and made his way into Parisian high society. The death of his mother in 1905 ended his career as a socialite. He became a recluse, spending most of his life in a soundproof, cork-lined room in his Paris apartment. There he wrote his great autobiographical novel *A la recherche du temps perdu* (*Remembrance of Things Past*). The first volume, *Swann's Way*, was turned down by France's top publishers and was printed at the author's expense in 1913. However, the second volume, *Within a Budding Grove*, won the Prix Goncourt in 1919 and established Proust's enduring reputation. The last six volumes of the novel were published posthumously.

Mary Quant
b. 1934

English fashion designer Mary Quant was one of the leading lights of the "Swinging London" scene of the 1960s. After leaving art college in 1955, she opened a small boutique called Bazaar in London's King's Road. With her husband, Alexander Plunket Greene, she specialized in cheap, ready-to-wear clothes for teenagers. In the early 1960s, her bold black-and-white geometrical designs took the youth market by storm. By 1963 her products were selling in 150 outlets in Britain and twice that number in the United States. She initiated a fashion revolution, establishing that young women would no longer dress like their mothers, and that fashion would be what was worn by young people on the street, rather than the creations of Parisian *haute couture*. It is disputed whether she actually created the mini-skirt, the most famous of all 1960s fashions, but she certainly popularized it. In the 1970s, she expanded into make-up and accessories.

Emperor Pu-yi
1906–67

Pu-yi was the last emperor of China. He ascended to the Chinese imperial throne in 1908 at the age of two, taking the dynastic name Hsuan T'ung. In 1912, however, he was forced to abdicate as a revolution created a new Chinese Republic. Pu-yi was given a pension and continued to live in the imperial palace in Beijing with extensive privileges. His presence served as a focus for the opponents of the republic, who restored him to the throne for twelve days in 1917. Deposed for a second time, he remained in Beijing until 1924, when he was evicted from the palace and fled to seek the protection of the Japanese. In 1932, Japan made him the nominal ruler of Manchukuo, the puppet state set up by the Japanese in Manchuria. Two years later, the Japanese allowed him to declare himself emperor once again, adopting the imperial name Kang Teh. Pu-yi was totally dependent on Japanese support, and the defeat of Japan by the United States and its allies in 1945 brought about his downfall. Manchuria was occupied by the Soviet Union and Pu-yi was arrested. The Soviet authorities later handed him over to the Communist rulers of China and he underwent a long process of "re-education" before his release in 1959. He worked at a machine repair shop in a Beijing botanical garden until his death in 1967.

Yitzhak Rabin
1922–95

Israeli soldier and statesman Yitzhak Rabin was born in Jerusalem and brought up in Tel Aviv. He rose to be chief of staff of the Israeli armed forces in 1964, leading them to victory in the Six-Day War of 1967. After serving as ambassador to the United States, he moved into politics, becoming leader of the Israeli Labour Party in 1974. As Israeli prime minister in 1993 he signed a peace agreement with the Palestine Liberation Organization (PLO), granting self-rule to the Palestinians in Gaza and the West Bank. In 1994, he was awarded the Nobel Peace Prize jointly with Palestinian leader Yasser Arafat and Israeli foreign minister Shimon Peres. Rabin was assassinated in 1995 by an Israeli extremist.

Satyajit Ray
1921–92

The distinguished Indian film director Satyajit Ray was born in Calcutta. He worked for an advertising agency and as a book illustrator before completing his first film, *Pather Panchali*, in 1955. Like most of his movies, it was made in Bengali. An award-winner at the Cannes Film Festival, it established Ray as a director of international stature. Together with *Aparajito* and *Apur Sansar*, it forms the Apu Trilogy, perhaps his finest work. Ray continued to direct movies throughout his life, although his output declined in the 1980s because of illness. He also wrote children's stories, poems, and novels, including a series featuring Feluda, a young Indian version of Sherlock Holmes.

KEY RAY FILMS

1955	*Pather Panchali (Father Panchali)*
1956	*Aparajito (The Unvanquished)*
1958	*Jalsaghar (The Music Room)*
1959	*Apur Sansar (The World of Apu)*
1964	*Mahanagar (The Big City)*
1965	*Charulata (The Lonely Wife)*
1970	*Aranyer din Ratri (Days and Nights in the Forest)*
1973	*Ashanti Sanket (Distant Thunder)*
1977	*Shatranj ke Khilari (The Chess Players)*
1992	*Agantuk (The Visitor)*

Auguste Rodin
1840–1917

French sculptor Auguste Rodin had a profound influence on 20th-century art. He was born into a poor family in Paris, and began training as an artist at 14. He failed three times to get into art school, however, and made his living as a stonemason. His life was transformed by a visit to Italy in 1875, where he was inspired by the sculpture of the Renaissance artist Michelangelo. He began to model clay and wax shapes, which were then cast in bronze. In 1878 he completed his first major work, *The Age of Bronze*, and in 1880 was commissioned to create a bronze door for a Paris art museum. Rodin worked on this vast project, called *The Gates of Hell*, for 20 years but it was never finished. His most celebrated masterpieces include *The Kiss* (1898) and *The Burghers of Calais* (1885–95). Rodin's massive, passionate figures were so realistic and powerful that they revived sculpture as a major art form.

Like most of Rodin's works, The Thinker is cast in bronze.

The Thinker
Rodin's famous sculpture *Le Penseur* (*The Thinker*) was originally created as part of *The Gates of Hell*, the bronze door for the Paris Museum of Decorative Arts that he worked on from 1880 to 1900, but never completed. It shows the love of muscular human form that Rodin had learned from the example of Michelangelo.

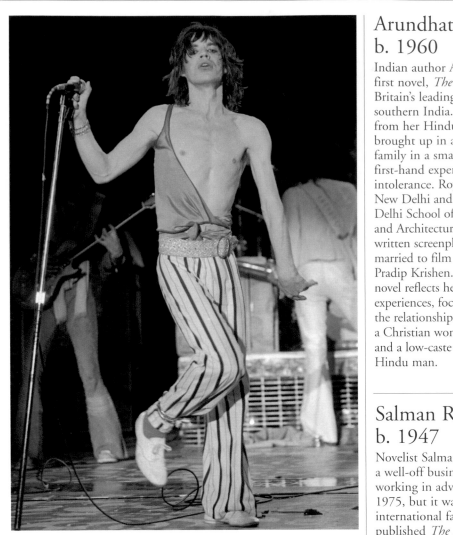

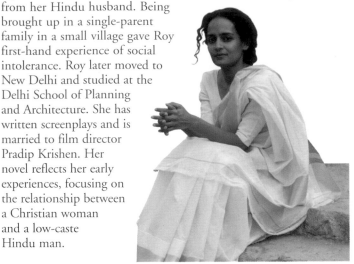

Arundhati Roy
b. 1960

Indian author Arundhati Roy shot to fame in 1997 when her first novel, *The God of Small Things*, won the Booker Prize, Britain's leading literary award. Roy was born in Kerala, southern India. Her mother, a Christian teacher, was separated from her Hindu husband. Being brought up in a single-parent family in a small village gave Roy first-hand experience of social intolerance. Roy later moved to New Delhi and studied at the Delhi School of Planning and Architecture. She has written screenplays and is married to film director Pradip Krishen. Her novel reflects her early experiences, focusing on the relationship between a Christian woman and a low-caste Hindu man.

Salman Rushdie
b. 1947

Novelist Salman Rushdie was born in Bombay, India, the son of a well-off businessman. He emigrated to Britain in 1965. After working in advertising, he published his first novel, *Grimus*, in 1975, but it was *Midnight's Children*, in 1981, which won him international fame and the prestigious Booker Prize. In 1988 he published *The Satanic Verses*, a novel which some Muslims claimed blasphemed Islam. As a result, a *fatwa* (death sentence) was issued against him by the Iranian leader Ayatollah Khomeini. With a bounty of $6,000,000 on his head, Rushdie went into hiding, under police protection. In 1998 the *fatwa* was officially withdrawn by the government of Iran, but Rushdie remained at risk from extremists.

KEY BOOKS BY RUSHDIE

1975	*Grimus* (novel)
1981	*Midnight's Children* (novel)
1983	*Shame* (novel)
1987	*The Jaguar Smile: A Nicaraguan Journey* (travel writing)
1988	*The Satanic Verses* (novel)
1990	*Haroun and the Sea of Stories* (novel)
1991	*Imaginary Homelands* (essays and criticism)
1994	*East, West* (short stories)
1995	*The Moor's Last Sigh* (novel)
1999	*The Ground Beneath Her Feet* (novel)

Rushdie recently won the "Booker of Bookers" prize for Midnight's Children.

The Rolling Stones
1962–

The Rolling Stones gave their first performance in London in July 1962. The group soon settled into the line-up of Mick Jagger (b. 1943), Keith Richards (b. 1943), Charlie Watts (b. 1941), Brian Jones (1944–69), and Bill Wyman (b. 1936). By 1965 their fresh version of rhythm and blues had won them worldwide fame with hit singles such as "Satisfaction" and "Get Off of My Cloud". The Stones were deliberately marketed as the "bad boys" of pop music, and Jagger and Richards were convicted on a drugs charge in 1967. Two years later, Brian Jones left the group, dying shortly afterwards. Mick Taylor (b. 1948) took his place until 1974, when he was replaced by Ron Wood (b. 1947). From the 1970s, Jagger became one of the international jet set, carrying on widely publicized relationships with a series of glamorous women. Although their later records fell short of the quality of those of the 1960s, the Stones continued to tour the globe as the self-styled "greatest rock 'n' roll band in the world".

KEY RECORDINGS

1963	"Come On" (single)
1964	"It's All Over Now" (single)
1965	"Satisfaction" (single)
1965	"Get Off of My Cloud" (single)
1966	*Aftermath* (album)
1968	"Jumping Jack Flash" (single)
1968	*Beggar's Banquet* (album)
1969	*Let It Bleed* (album)
1969	"Honky Tonk Women" (single)
1971	*Sticky Fingers* (album)
1976	*Black and Blue* (album)
1978	*Some Girls* (album)
1981	*Tatoo You* (album)

Amartya Sen
b. 1933

Economist Amartya Sen was born in Shantiniketan, India, and educated at Presidency College, Calcutta, and Trinity College, Cambridge. He taught at the Delhi School of Economics from 1963 to 1971 and then spent time at the London School of Economics, Oxford University, and Harvard before taking the post of Master of Trinity College, Cambridge, reputedly the most prestigious academic position in Britain. His radical work on the root causes of poverty and famine, and their relationship to social inequality, earned him the Nobel Prize for economic sciences in 1998. Sen's most influential book is *Poverty and Famines: An Essay on Entitlement and Deprivation*, published in 1981.

Vikram Seth
b. 1952

Indian poet and novelist Vikram Seth was born into a wealthy family in Calcutta – his mother was the first woman in India to become a high court judge. Seth studied economics at Oxford University in England and Stanford University in the United States, but then decided that his future lay in writing rather than a career as an economist. He lived in China for two years and was deeply influenced by classical Chinese poetry. He published his own first book of poems, *Mappings*, in 1980, and wrote a book about his travels in China, *From Heaven Lake*. His breakthrough came in 1986 with the publication of *Golden Gate*, a novel about life in California written entirely in rhyming verse. With his reputation established, Seth moved to Delhi to live with his parents and work on an even more ambitious work, *A Suitable Boy*, published in 1993 to international acclaim. His next novel, *An Equal Music*, which appeared in 1999, centred around the life of a violinist, demonstrating once more the surprising range of Seth's talents and interests.

KEY BOOKS BY SETH

1980	*Mappings* (poems)
1983	*From Heaven Lake* (travel)
1985	*The Humble Administrator's Garden* (poems)
1986	*The Golden Gate* (novel in verse)
1990	*All You Who Sleep Tonight* (poems)
1991	*Beastly Tales from Here and There* (poems)
1992	*Three Chinese Poets* (poems)
1993	*A Suitable Boy* (novel)
1999	*An Equal Music* (novel)

A Suitable Boy

A Suitable Boy is reputed to be the longest single-volume novel ever written in English. The story of a young woman's search for the right husband set against the background of Indian politics in the early years of independence, it was an international bestseller and confirmed Seth as one of the leading writers of his generation.

Ravi Shankar
b. 1920

Born in Benares (Varanasi), India, musician Ravi Shankar began his career as a member of a travelling company run by his brother Uday. After an intensive period of study of Indian classical music, he emerged in the 1950s as the world's leading player of the sitar. He was responsible for introducing the instrument to Western audiences and became a major influence on 1960s pop music. He taught Beatle George Harrison to play the sitar and performed at pop festivals himself. He also developed a fruitful collaboration with leading Western classical musicians, especially the violinist Yehudi Menuhin. Since the 1970s, Shankar has been less prominent, but he has continued to be influential, encouraging the development of the "world music" movement.

KEY CAREER DATES

1957	Makes his first tour of the United States.
1965	Records *Portrait of a Genius*.
1966	Records *Menuhin Meets Shankar* with violinist Yehudi Menuhin.
1967	Performs at the Monterey Pop Festival.
1969	Performs at the Woodstock festival.
1996	Records *In Celebration*.

O.J. Simpson
b. 1947

Orenthal James Simpson, universally known as "O.J.", was possibly the greatest running back in the history of American football, but his sporting fame was later eclipsed by his involvement in one of America's most sensational murder cases. Born in San Francisco, California, Simpson was the leading collegiate footballer of 1968 and joined the Buffalo Bills the following year. In 1973, he established a new rushing record of 2,003 yards and was voted Most Valued Player for the season. He left the Buffalo Bills for the San Francisco 49ers in 1978, but retired soon afterwards. Simpson's prowess on the field was matched by his good looks and personal charm, and he soon became one of the leading African-American media personalities.

However, Simpson's marriage to Nicole Brown was not a success and ended in divorce. In 1994, Nicole Brown Simpson and her friend Ronald Goldman were brutally murdered. Simpson was charged with the killings, but cleared by a jury after a nine-month court case in October 1995. The controversial verdict failed to clear his name in the eyes of many Americans. In February 1997, the families of the victims successfully sued Simpson for causing wrongful death and were awarded $8.5 million in damages.

Court controversy
The murder trial of O.J. Simpson, held in Los Angeles from January to October 1995, gripped the attention of the American media. The prosecution of Simpson for killing his ex-wife Nicole Brown Simpson and her friend Ronald Goldman was based largely on what was apparently overwhelming forensic evidence. However, Simpson's defence concentrated on racial issues, trying to convince the predominantly African-American jury that Simpson had been framed by racist Los Angeles police officers. In its view of the case, the American public was largely split along ethnic lines. Most African-Americans agreed with the jury in finding Simpson not guilty, while most white Americans held that he should have been found guilty of the killings.

Key Spielberg movies	
1971	*Duel* (TV Movie)
1975	*Jaws*
1977	*Close Encounters of the Third Kind*
1981	*Raiders of the Lost Ark*
1982	*E.T. The Extra-Terrestrial*
1985	*The Color Purple*
1987	*Empire of the Sun*
1989	*Indiana Jones and the Last Crusade*
1993	*Jurassic Park*
1993	*Schindler's List*
1997	*Amistad*
1998	*Saving Private Ryan*

Steven Spielberg
b. 1947

Steven Spielberg ranks as the most commercially successful director in cinema history – many of his movies are among the highest-grossing ever made. Spielberg was born in Cincinnati, Ohio. He decided as a child that he wanted a career in the film industry and started making movies while still at school, shooting his first amateur film with a script and actors at the age of 12. After studying film at California State College, he began directing TV movies in the early 1970s, and made his first feature, *The Sugarland Express*, in 1974. His first big success came the following year with *Jaws*, a low-budget movie that broke all box-office records. By the early 1980s, Spielberg was the most successful film maker in Hollywood and was branching out into production as well as directing. His films were admired for providing family entertainment, but he aspired to make more serious movies on social themes. The first of these was *The Color Purple*, based on the novel by Alice Walker, in 1985. He won an Oscar for Best Director for his Holocaust film, *Schindler's List*, in 1993. He has continued to alternate blockbuster entertainment movies, such as the immensely successful *Jurassic Park* (1993), with serious dramas, such as *Amistad* (1997), a film about the slave trade, and the much-admired war epic *Saving Private Ryan*, which won him his second Oscar for Best Director.

Shark blockbuster
Steven Spielberg was a young unknown when Universal Studios entrusted him with directing his second feature film, *Jaws,* based on a bestselling novel by Peter Benchley. Released in 1975, it tells the tale of a shark terrorizing a New England beach town. It cost a modest $8.5 million to make, but became the highest-earning movie produced up to that time. *Jaws* not only made Spielberg's career, but also changed the face of Hollywood. It started the era of "blockbuster" movies, packed with thrills and special effects, and designed to attract the youth audience.

DreamWorks
In 1994, Spielberg joined forces with Hollywood moguls Jeffrey Katzenberg and David Geffen to form DreamWorks, a multimedia entertainment studio. Among the first DreamWorks productions were the thrillers *The Peacemaker* and *Deep Impact*, and the computer-animated comedy *Antz*.

Marie Stopes
1880–1958

British birth-control pioneer Marie Stopes was born in Edinburgh, Scotland. After studying at University College, London, and in Munich, Stopes became the first female science lecturer at Manchester University, where she taught fossil botany. When her first marriage broke down in 1914, she focused her attention on marital problems caused by ignorance and began to campaign for more public information about contraception. Her most important book, *Married Love*, a guide to sex and marriage, was published in 1918 and sold over 400,000 copies in its first five years in print. Although many people welcomed her honesty, some were shocked at her openness about sex and birth control. The book was immediately banned as obscene in the United States. Undeterred, Stopes opened the first British birth-control clinic in north London in 1921, with the support of her second husband, Humphrey Verdon Roe. In 1930, with other campaigners, she founded the National Birth Control Council, which became the Family Planning Association in 1939. By that time, the organization was running over 60 clinics in Britain. Stopes was a prolific writer, publishing more than 70 books and pamphlets.

KEY DATES

1904 Receives a doctorate in Munich, Germany, for work on plant fossils.

1911 Marries Reginald Ruggles Gates.

1914 Marriage annulled.

1918 Marries Humphrey Verdon Roe and publishes *Married Love* and *Wise Parenthood*.

1921 Founds Britain's first family-planning clinic.

1930 National Birth Control Council is created.

Rabindranath Tagore
1861–1941

Indian writer and philosopher Rabindranath Tagore published his first book of poetry at the age of 17. In 1901, he started a school, the *Santiniketan*, to combine the cultures of East and West. It later became the Visva-Bharati University. His books include the novel *Binodini* (1902), and *Gitanjali* (1912), a collection of religious verse. He was awarded the Nobel Prize for literature in 1913. Tagore was knighted by the British in 1915, but resigned the knighthood after the Amritsar Massacre of 1919, in which British troops opened fire on unarmed Indian demonstrators.

Pyotr Ilyich Tchaikovsky
1840–93

Russian composer Pyotr Ilyich Tchaikovsky was born in Kamsko-Votkinsk. He studied law and became a civil servant in 1859, but went to study music at the St. Petersburg Conservatory in 1863. He then became a professor at the new Moscow Conservatory. He first achieved public renown with his Symphony No. 2 (1872), the Piano Concerto No. 1 (1875), and operas using Russian folk tunes. Tchaikovsky's disastrous short-lived marriage to Antonina Ivanovna Miliukova in 1877 led to a nervous breakdown, and he composed little in the next few years. He toured Europe and the United States as a conductor, but sank into depression after Nadezhda von Meck, who had helped to finance his composing, stopped his allowance. He died, probably by suicide, in 1893. His music includes six symphonies, three ballets, and ten operas.

KEY WORKS

1868 *Romeo and Juliet* (overture)

1875 Piano Concerto No. 1 in B flat minor

1876 *Swan Lake* (ballet)

1878 Violin Concerto in D

1879 *Eugene Onégin* (opera)

1880 *1812 Overture*

1885 *Manfred Symphony* (tone-poem)

1888 Symphony No. 5 in E minor

1889 *Sleeping Beauty* (ballet)

1890 *The Queen of Spades* (opera)

1892 *The Nutcracker* (ballet)

1893 Symphony No. 6 in B minor, the *Pathétique*

Sachin Tendulkar
b. 1973

The Indian cricketer Sachin Ramesh Tendulkar was born into a middle-class family in the suburbs of Bombay. Under the guidance of his brother he developed into a competent bowler and a highly effective right-hand batsman. While still playing as a schoolboy in the local Ranji Trophy, he came to the attention of the top Indian cricketer Sunil Gavaskar, who became his godfather and encouraged him to take up the game at a professional level. Tendulkar made his test debut in 1989, and since then he has become a major force in the world of cricket. Small in stature, Tendulkar is a flamboyant batsman who attempts to dominate bowlers at all times. This attitude has endeared him to Indian cricket enthusiasts, who regard him with near veneration.

TENDULKAR HIGHLIGHTS

1989 Makes his test debut against Pakistan at the age of 16.

1994 Scores 179 runs in match against the West Indies at Nagpur in India.

1995 Signs a massive sponsorship deal with the US-based WorldTel organization which is reputedly worth US $7.5 million.

1998 Scores an unbeaten 204 runs against Australia in Bombay – a career best.

1999 Scores an unbeaten 140 against Kenya in the one-day World Cup series in England.

Margaret Thatcher
b. 1925

KEY CAREER DATES

1975 Replaces Edward Heath as leader of the Conservative party.

1979 Becomes Britain's first ever woman prime minister.

1983 Wins second general election, her large majority a consequence of success in the 1982 Falklands war.

1987 Elected for a third consecutive term, despite a reduced majority in the House of Commons.

1990 Forced to resign because of Conservative disquiet over the introduction of the poll tax and her anti-European views.

Trained first as a chemist and then a barrister, Margaret Hilda Thatcher entered Parliament as MP for Finchley in 1959, before serving as secretary of state for education (1970–74). Following the Conservative defeat in 1974, she was chosen to replace Edward Heath as party leader, and won the first of three consecutive general elections in 1979. As prime minister, Thatcher pursued right-wing policies which included privatization of state institutions (such as British Gas, British Airways and Rolls-Royce), the introduction of anti-trade union legislation, and the imposition of tighter controls over local government. At the same time, she attempted to curb government spending, but in this she was singularly unsuccessful, especially in the light of increased welfare payments as a consequence of high levels of unemployment. In international affairs, Thatcher established a reputation for her forthright criticism of the Soviet Union – where she was known as the "Iron Lady" – and with her close ally Ronald Reagan she did much to increase the tempo of the cold war. Her style of government became increasingly autocratic in the late 1980s, and growing dissent within the Conservative party forced her to resign. Subsequently, she established herself in a new career as an elder stateswoman, propounding her trenchant views to a worldwide audience.

Urban exhorts the assembly to fight Islam.

Pope Urban II
1035–99

The French pope responsible for instigating the crusades, Urban became a monk at the great monastery of Cluny. After serving as a bishop and cardinal, he was elected pope in 1088. He held a great meeting in 1095 outside the city of Clermont and called upon Europe's feudal nobility to go on a crusade, or holy war, to capture Jerusalem from the Muslims. As many as 130,000 people set off on the crusade, which culminated in the storming of Jerusalem in 1099 and the massacre of most of its inhabitants. This marked the beginning of centuries of conflict between Christians and Muslims.

Vincent Van Gogh
1853–90

The Dutch post-impressionist painter Vincent Van Gogh was born in Groot-Zundert in the Netherlands, the son of a Protestant pastor. After leaving school he worked in a variety of occupations before moving to Belgium to become an itinerant preacher. In 1881 his interest in painting led him to begin formal studies in Brussels, although shortly afterwards he returned to the Netherlands where he painted grim studies of domestic poverty. Van Gogh's art-dealer brother Theo provided funds for him to study in Paris, and there he met leading impressionist painters who included Toulouse-Lautrec and Gauguin. In 1888 he travelled to the south of France, where

landscape and bright sunshine provided him with the inspiration to paint his great masterpieces. The wild expressiveness of Van Gogh's painting was paralleled by a deep inner turbulence, which led him to cut off part of his ear in a fit of remorse after threatening his friend Gauguin during a quarrel. He was sent to a local asylum before being placed under the supervision of a sympathetic physician, Dr. Gachet, but suffering acute depression he shot himself. Van Gogh's exuberant use of colour was to have a profound and lasting influence on the course of 20th-century art.

VAN GOGH'S LIFE

1869 Works as an assistant to an international art dealer with offices in The Hague, London, and Paris.

1876 Travels to England, where he works as a teacher and attempts to train as a Methodist minister.

1885 Paints *The Potato Eaters*, a group of poor peasants from his father's parish – his first major work.

1886 Resumes his art studies in Paris and paints some 200 pictures during a two-year stay.

1888 Moves to Arles, where he paints such classics as *Sunflowers*, *The Bridge*, and *The Chair and the Pipe*.

1890 Completes last work, *Cornfields with Flight of Birds*, before returning to the scene to commit suicide.

A Van Gogh is sold at auction.

Van Gogh's art
Van Gogh's great outpouring of artistic achievement took place over two years (1888–90) in the south of France, and included many self-portraits, such as the example above. Although he was admired by some of his fellow painters, it was only at the end of his life that he began to gain some critical attention from the art world. But the rough and emotionally raw nature of his compositions found little favour among the art collectors of the period.

Posthumous reputation
Tragically, only one of Van Gogh's paintings was sold in his lifetime, a sale that was made by his brother Theo, who provided both financial and emotional support for Vincent. During the 20th century, Van Gogh's reputation was transformed – as were the prices of his paintings. His 1890 painting *Irises* reached a price of $53.9 million when it was sold at auction in New York in 1987, the highest price that had ever been paid for a work.

Kath Walker
1920–93

The Australian Aboriginal writer and poet Kath (Kathleen Jean) Walker was born in Queensland, Australia, and grew up with the Noonnuccal tribe on Stradbroke Island. After working as a domestic servant she spent the war years in the Australian Army Women's Service. She was an early pioneer in the campaign for Aboriginal rights, and her writing reflected these beliefs. In 1964 she brought out *We Are Going*, the first book of poetry to be published by an Aboriginal writer. It sold out in three days. Among her other publications were *The Dawn Is at Hand* (1966), *Stradbroke Dreamtime* (1972), *Father Sky and Mother Earth* (1981), and *The Rainbow Serpent* (1988). In 1967 she was involved in the campaign that gave Aboriginals constitutional recognition for the first time. In 1988 she adopted the Aboriginal name Oodgeroo Noonnuccal.

A protest march by Aborigines for land rights

William Wallace
1272–1305

William Wallace is remembered as one of Scotland's greatest national heroes. In 1297, he led a rebellion against King Edward I of England, who had conquered much of Scotland and expelled the Scottish king. Wallace gathered an army and defeated the English troops at the battle of Stirling Bridge. He then moved south to attack England's border counties. But Wallace's triumph was short-lived. In 1298, Edward defeated him at Falkirk. Wallace went into hiding, and in 1299 travelled to France to seek support for the Scottish cause. Returning in 1303, he waged a guerrilla war against the English. He was eventually captured and executed as a common criminal by hanging, drawing, and quartering.

Andy Warhol
1928–87

American artist Andy Warhol was born in Pennsylvania. He moved to New York in 1949 and made a successful career as a commercial artist working in advertising. In 1962, he exhibited pictures of Campbell's soup cans and Brillo soap-pad boxes, and was soon recognized as a leader of the Pop Art movement. Scorning the traditional values of craftsmanship and self-expression associated with high art, he mass-produced pictures in his New York studio, which he called the Factory. Using silk-screen printing, he manufactured many repeated images of icons of popular culture such as Marilyn Monroe and Elvis Presley. He was also an avant-garde film maker. One of his most famous movies, *Sleep* (1965), shows a man sleeping for six hours. In 1965, he moved into rock music, promoting the group the Velvet Underground. In 1968, he was shot and seriously wounded by Valerie Solanas, founder of the Society for Cutting Up Men (SCUM). Warhol was as well-known for his strange personality and for his quotable sayings as he was for his art.

WARHOL QUOTES

"I like making movies because it's easier than painting paintings."

"I want everybody to think alike. I think everybody should be a machine."

"In the future everyone will be famous for 15 minutes."

"An artist is someone who produces things that people don't need to have but that he – for some reason – thinks it would be a good idea to give them."

Mary Wollstonecraft
1759–97

The British feminist and writer Mary Wollstonecraft was born in London, the daughter of Anglo-Irish parents. She spent her early working life as a teacher, governess, and translator. Through her work she became involved with a group of political reformers called the English Jacobins, whose members included the radical writers Thomas Paine and William Godwin, and the visionary poet William Blake. In 1792, Wollstonecraft moved to Paris, in order to witness at first hand the dramatic upheavals of the French Revolution. While she was there, she met an American, Captain Gilbert Imlay, by whom she had a daughter. In the same year, Wollstonecraft wrote her most famous work, *Vindication of the Rights of Woman*, in which she called for the social equality of the sexes and equal opportunities for women in education. Her ideas were radical for their time, and her book is now seen as an early feminist classic. In 1797 Wollstonecraft married William Godwin. Their daughter, Mary, later married the poet Shelley and wrote the classic Gothic novel *Frankenstein*.

FEMINIST CLASSICS

1792 *Vindication of the Rights of Woman*, Mary Wollstonecraft

1869 *The Subjection of Women*, John Stuart Mill

1929 *A Room of One's Own*, Virginia Woolf

1949 *The Second Sex*, Simone de Beauvoir

1963 *The Feminine Mystique*, Betty Friedan

1970 *The Female Eunuch*, Germaine Greer

Sir Christopher Wren
1632–1723

Sir Christopher Wren is generally held to have been the greatest of English architects. Born in Wiltshire, in his early years Wren showed promise as a scientist. After distinguishing himself at Oxford University in the study of mathematics and physics, he became a professor of astronomy and was a founding member of the Royal Society in 1660. His growing interest in architecture was helped by his knowledge of practical geometry. He designed or restored several of the major buildings in the university cities of Cambridge and Oxford, including Oxford's Sheldonian Theatre (1669). After much of London was destroyed by the Great Fire of 1666, Wren drew up grandiose plans for rebuilding the whole city, but these were not carried out. He did, however, redesign more than 50 London churches, the most famous being the graceful columns, arches, and domes of St. Paul's Cathedral (1675–1710). Wren created many of London's other most famous landmarks – among his masterpieces are Chelsea Hospital (1691) and Greenwich Hospital (1715).

Guggenheim Museum of Art

Frank Lloyd Wright
1867–1959

Wisconsin-born American architect Frank Lloyd Wright first set up his own practice in Chicago in 1893. His early designs were for "prairie" homes such as the Willits House (1902) and the Robie House (1909–10). He believed that buildings should seem to grow organically out of the landscape, and gave them long, low proportions. In 1915 he began work on the Imperial Hotel in Tokyo, which was one of the few big buildings to survive the earthquake of 1923. In the 1930s, Wright developed the use of modern materials such as pre-cast concrete blocks. His design for the Fallingwater house in Pennsylvania (1936–37) featured concrete balconies suspended above a waterfall. His last major work was the Guggenheim Museum of Art in New York (1959), in which paintings are exhibited along a single spiral ramp.

Emile Zola
1840–1902

The French novelist Emile Zola was born in Paris. His family was often short of money and, as a young man, he lived in real poverty during two years of unemployment. After a spell as a journalist, he published his first fictional work, a collection of short stories, in 1864. He became a member of the circle of writers gathered around the novelist Gustave Flaubert and propounded a theory of the novel known as "naturalism". This asserted that "the novelist should observe and record dispassionately – like the scientist". His chief literary achievement, the 20-volume family saga *Les Rougon-Macquart*, began to appear in 1867. It purported to show the effect of heredity and environment on different members of a single family, as well as painting a sweeping portrait of the degeneracy and social injustice of France under the Second Empire (1852–70). The series includes *Nana* (1880), the story of a courtesan, *Germinal* (1885), about a miners' strike, and *La Terre* (1887), a harsh view of French peasant life. The last volume of the series, *Le Docteur Pascal*, appeared in 1893. Zola's work declined in the last decade of his life. He died from carbon-monoxide poisoning as a result of a blocked chimney.

The Dreyfus case

In 1894, a Jewish officer, Captain Alfred Dreyfus, was wrongly convicted of spying by a French military court and sentenced to solitary confinement on Devil's Island. It slowly became clear that Dreyfus had been framed. In 1898, Zola published an open letter, headlined "J'accuse" ("I Accuse"), denouncing the authorities for injustice. The government responded by prosecuting Zola, who was forced to flee to England to escape prison. Dreyfus was pardoned in 1899, although his name was not finally cleared until 1906.

Captain Dreyfus with his wife and children

REFERENCE

In a rapidly changing world, facts and figures need continual updating to keep pace with developments. These two pages give the latest available statistics for population and national wealth, and bring some essential lists of prizewinners and records up-to-date.

World population 1998

Region	Population
Africa	748,927,000
Asia	3,585,372,000
Australasia and Oceania	29,644,000
Central and South America	503,524,000
Europe	728,871,000
North America	304,716,000
World population total	5,901,054,000

The world population, which reached 3 billion in 1960, was expected to pass 6 billion in 1999. Current projections suggest that in 2050 the world population will total 8.9 billion, as the rate of growth slows.

Some of the 1.2 billion citizens of China

Highest population 1998
The five countries with the highest populations included three Asian states, China, India, and Indonesia.

Country	Population
China	1,300,000,000
India	976,000,000
United States	274,000,000
Indonesia	206,000,000
Brazil	165,000,000

Lowest population 1998
The five countries with the lowest populations included three Pacific island states, Nauru, Tuvalu, and Palau.

Country	Population
Vatican	1,000
Tuvalu	10,000
Nauru	11,000
Palau	18,000
San Marino	25,000

National wealth

One way of comparing different countries' wealth or poverty is to divide their Gross Domestic Product (GDP) – their total economic output – by their population.

Richest countries 1997

Country	GDP per head in US$
Luxembourg	37,785
Liechtenstein	35,170
Switzerland	35,170
Norway	34,890
Japan	33,265
Denmark	30,718
United States	28,789
Singapore	28,107
Iceland	27,181
Sweden	25,718

Poorest countries 1997

Country	GDP per head in US$
Congo (Zaïre)	52
Sudan	59
Mozambique	94
Guinea-Bissau	96
Ethiopia	104
Madagascar	122
Burundi	126
Chad	149
Cambodia	159
Burkina Faso	160

South African leaders

South Africa's political leaders were its prime ministers until 1984, and presidents after that date.

1910–19	Louis Botha
1919–24	Jan Christian Smuts
1924–39	James Hertzog
1939–48	Jan Christian Smuts
1948–54	Daniel Malan
1954–58	Johannes Strijdom
1958–66	Hendrik Verwoerd
1966–78	B. J. Vorster
1978–89	P. W. Botha
1989–94	F. W. De Klerk
1994–99	Nelson Mandela
1999–	Thabo Mbeke

Thabo Mbeke

UN secretary generals

Kofi Annan

1946–52	Trygve Lie	Norwegian
1953–61	Dag Hammarskjold	Swedish
1961–71	U Thant	Burmese
1972–81	Kurt Waldheim	Austrian
1982–91	Javier Perez de Cuellar	Peruvian
1992–96	Boutros Boutros Ghali	Egyptian
1997–	Kofi Annan	Ghanain

Nobel prizewinners 1996–98

Physics
1996	David M. Lee, Douglas D. Osheroff, and Robert C. Richardson	Discovery of superfluidity in helium-3.
1997	Steven Chu, Claude Cohen-Tannoudji, and William D. Phillips	Developing methods to cool and trap atoms with laser light.
1998	Robert B. Laughlin, Horst L. Stormer, and Daniel C. Tsui	Discovering a new form of quantum fluid.

Chemistry
1996	Robert F. Curl, Jr., Sir Harold W. Kroto, and Richard E. Smalley	Discovery of fullerenes.
1997	Paul D. Boyer, John E. Walker, and Jens C. Skou	Work on enzymes.
1998	Walter Kohn and John A. Pople	Development of computational methods in quantum chemistry.

Literature
1996	Wislawa Szymborska	Polish poet.
1997	Dario Fo	Italian dramatist.
1998	Jose Saramago	Portuguese novelist.

Peace
1996	Carlos Felipe Ximenes Belo and José Ramos Horta	Helping to bring peace to the conflict in East Timor.
1997	International Campaign to Ban Landmines and Jody Williams	Campaign to ban anti-personnel mines.
1998	John Hume and David Trimble	Efforts to achieve peace in Northern Ireland.

Economic sciences
1996	James A. Mirrlees and William Vickrey	Economic theory of incentives under asymmetric information.
1997	Robert C. Merton and Myron S. Scholes	A new method to determine the value of derivatives.
1998	Amartya Sen	Contribution to welfare economics.

Physiology or medicine
1996	Peter C. Doherty and Rolf M. Zinkernagel	Discoveries concerning the specificity of the cell-mediated immune defence.
1997	Stanley B. Prusiner	Discovery of prions, a new biological principle of infection.
1998	Robert F. Furchgott, Louis J Ignarro, and Ferid Murad	Nitric oxide as a signalling molecule in the cardiovascular system.

RECENT SPORTING VICTORIES

COMPETITION	YEAR	WINNER
American Football Super Bowl	1997	Green Bay Packers
	1998	Denver Broncos
	1999	Denver Broncos
Football World Cup	1998	France
Baseball World Series	1997	Florida Marlins
	1998	New York Yankees
Formula 1 Championship	1997	Jacques Villeneuve (Canada)
	1998	Mika Hakkinen (Finland)

RECENT WINNERS OF TENNIS SINGLES

TOURNAMENT	1997	1998
French Open men's	Gustavo Kurten	Carlos Moya
French Open women's	Iva Majoli	Arantxa SanchezVicario
Australian Open men's	Pete Sampras	Petr Korda
Australian Open women's	Martina Hingis	Martina Hingis
US Open men's	Pat Rafter	Pat Rafter
US Open women's	Martina Hingis	Lindsay Davenport
Wimbledon men's	Pete Sampras	Pete Sampras
Wimbledon women's	Martina Hingis	Jana Novotna

RECENT WINNERS OF GOLF MAJORS

TOURNAMENT	1997	1998
US Masters	Tiger Woods	Mark O'Meara
US Open	Ernie Els	Lee Janzen
British Open	Justin Leonard	Mark O'Meara
US PGA	Davis Love III	Vijay Singh

NEW ATHLETICS RECORDS

Men

EVENT	YEAR	RECORD HOLDER	COUNTRY	RECORD
800 m	1997	Wilson Kipketer	Denmark	1 min 41.11 secs
1500 m	1998	Hicham El Guerouj	Morocco	3 mins 26 secs
3000 m	1997	Bernard Barmasai	Kenya	7 mins 55.72 secs
5000 m	1998	Haile Gebrselassie	Ethiopia	12 mins 39.36 secs
10,000 m	1998	Haile Gebrselassie	Ethiopia	26 mins 22.75 secs
Marathon	1998	Ronaldo da Costa	Brazil	2 hours 6 mins 5 secs
50 km walk	1996	Thierry Toutain	France	3 hours 40 mins 58 secs
4x400m	1998	United States team	USA	2 mins 54.20 secs

Women

EVENT	YEAR	RECORD HOLDER	COUNTRY	RECORD
5000 m	1997	Jiang Bo	China	14 mins 28.09 secs
Marathon	1998	Tegla Loroupe	Kenya	2 hours 20 mins 47 secs
Hammer throw	1998	Michaela Melinte	Romania	73.14 m

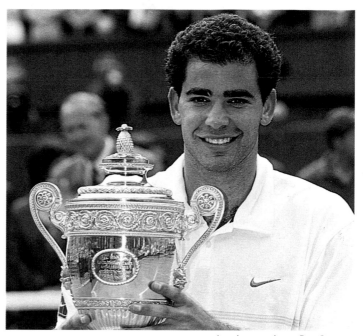

American tennis star Pete Sampras

HIGHEST-GROSSING MOVIES WORLDWIDE

FILM	YEAR	BOX-OFFICE RECEIPTS
Titanic	1997	$1,835,400,000
Jurassic Park	1993	$919,800,000
Independence Day	1996	$811,100,000
Star Wars	1977	$783,600,000
The Lion King	1994	$766,900,000
E.T. the Extra-Terrestrial	1982	$704,800,000
Forrest Gump	1994	$679,700,000
Lost World	1997	$614,100,000
Men In Black	1997	$586,100,000
Return of the Jedi	1983	$572,800,000

MOST OSCARS WON

FILM	YEAR	AWARDS
Ben-Hur	1959	11
Titanic	1997	11
Gigi	1958	9
The Last Emperor	1987	9
The English Patient	1996	9
Gone With the Wind	1939	8
From Here to Eternity	1953	8
On the Waterfront	1954	8
My Fair Lady	1964	8
Cabaret	1972	8
Gandhi	1982	8

Glark Gable in *Gone With the Wind*

BESTSELLING SINGLES WORLDWIDE

SINGLE	ARTIST
Candle in the Wind, 1997	Elton John
White Christmas	Bing Crosby
Rock around the Clock	Bill Haley and His Comets
I Want to Hold Your Hand	Beatles
It's Now or Never	Elvis Presley
I Will Always Love You	Whitney Houston
Don't Be Cruel/Hound Dog	Elvis Presley
Diana	Paul Anka

Elton John performs *Candle in the Wind* **at Princess Diana's funeral**

BESTSELLING ALBUMS

ALBUM	ARTIST
Thriller	Michael Jackson
Dark Side of the Moon	Pink Floyd
Bat out of Hell	Meat Loaf
The Bodyguard	Soundtrack
Saturday Night Fever	Soundtrack
Sgt. Pepper's Lonely Hearts Club Band	Beatles
The Eagles Greatest Hits 1971-75	Eagles
Music Box	Mariah Carey

INDEX

Main entries are referenced in **bold**.

PICTURE SOURCES

The publishers would like to thank the following for their permission to use their photographs:

Abbreviations:
a: above, b: below, c: centre, l: left, r: right, t: top

AKG London: 62tl, 89b **Allsport:** 5ar, Clive Brunskill 33tl, Pascal Rondeau 42bc, Ross Kinnaird 42bl, SOCOG 42cl **Ancient Art & Architecture Collection:** 35cl **Anglo-Australian Observatory:** 2 **Art Directors and Trip Photo Library:** D.P. Anerjee 37tr, Dinodia 38bc, Eric Smith 31cr, F. Good 35tr, H Rogers 35bl, 37bl, 38br, M MacKenzie 50cl, Terry Why 48cl **Barnaby's Picture Library:** 54ac, Bill Meadows 53cr, Brian Gibbs 32t, David Young 50acr **John Bethell:** 45bl **Blists Hill Museum/DK Picture Library:** Andy Crawford 54bc **Bridgeman Art Library, London & New York:** Belvoir Castle, Leicestershire 45tr, City of Bristol Museum and Art Gallery 46tl, Forbes Magazine Collection, New York 53cl, National Portrait Gallery, London 45cr, 46tr, Philip Mould, Historical Portraits Ltd, London, UK 81cr, Phillips, The International Fine Art Auctioneers 45tl, Private Collection 40cl, 40bl, 45br, 85br, Richard Philip, London 45cl, Trades Union Congress, London 54bcl, Victoria & Albert Museum, London 44ac, Wallace Collection, London 46br **British Museum, London:** 47cl **British Red Cross:** 43bcl **Camera Press:** 47cr, Jon Blau 32bl, Martine Velon 29tl **The J. Allan Cash Photolibrary:** 33tr, 33cr, 33b, 55cr **Collections:** Roger Scruton 33bc **Colorific!:** Terence Spencer 44ar **Corbis UK Ltd:** 52bl, 52bfl, 52cb, 52clb, 52cflb, 52cfr, 52c,

52cfl, 52cla, 52cl, 52tfr, 52tr, 52tc, 52tl, 52tfl, 52ca, 52cfra, Bettmann 48t, 49tr, 60tl, 65t, 68bl, 68t, 73bl, 75bl, 76tr, 82bc, 83br, 90b, 92c, 93tr, Charles Harris 49tc, Hulton Getty 51bc, Hulton-Deutsch Collection 64b, 69c, 80c, 82tr, 84bl, 93br, Jim Lake 88t, Joseph Sohm, ChromoSohm Inc 50br, Karan Kapoor 86tr, Mark Stephenson 64cr, Matthew Mendelsohn 86b, Neal Preston 86tl, Pennie Tweedie 91b, Scott Wachter 74br, Sean Aidan/Eye Ubiquitous 63br, Ted Streshinsky 87br, Vittoriano Rastelli 61tr, Wally McNamee 56bl **DK Picture Library:** 37tc, 38bl, 42cr, 56c, 56by, Geoff Brightling 39cr, Andy Crawford 50bc, Exeter Museum/David Garner 57bc, Steve Gorton 44br, Paul Harris 55tr, Barnabas Kindersley 37bl, Dave King 38cl, 50t, Liz Mcaulay 46cl, 55c, 55br, Stephen Oliver 33br, Kim Sayer 36bcr, **The English Heritage Photo Library:** 46tc **E.T. Archive:** 40cr, 53bl, 90c **Mary Evans Picture Library:** 31bl, 31tl, 43c, 52cfla, 52cra, 54tl, 54tr, 54bcr, 63t, 63c, 64tr, 68br, 69br, 76bl, 78c, 79b, 79t, 81tl, 81cl, 83tr, 84t, 85bc, 89t, 92t, 93tl, 93bl, Edward Tilt, Illustrated London News 57tl, Illustrated London News 54acl, Valentine & Sons 53br **Ffotograff:** Charles Aithie 55tl **Fortean Picture Library:** Janet and Colin Bord 55cl **Fotomedia:** T.C Jain 37tl G2 Film Trial by Fire Films Dilip Mehta 36bl **Ronald Grant Archive:** 66c, 70tr, 71tl, 73tr, 75tl, 77tc, 82br, 88br **Royal Green Jackets Museum/DK Geoff Dann:** 54br **Robert Harding Picture Library:** 21, 22, 57cl, A Woolfitt 25, E Simanor 20, Fraser Hall 23, Rob Francis 30tl **Roger de la Harpe:** 57c, 57bl, 57br **Hulton Getty:** 31tr, 40t, 46bl, 64tl, 78b, 84br, 92b **Hyphen Films Ltd:**

Collection Nasreen Munni Kabir 62c **Images of India:** Marcus Grover 35tc **Image Bank:** Jeff Hunter 30tr, Patti McConville 48bl **Impact Photos:** Ben Edwards 37bcr **Katz Pictures:** Gerry Gropp/Time 48cr, Graeme Williams 28b, 57tr, Steve Liss/Time 48br **Kobal Collection:** 33cl, 85t **Frank Lane Picture Agency:** David Hosking 38cr **Magnum:** G. Mendel 29tr, Abbas 28cl, 34cr, Bruno Barbey 36cr, Cartier-Bresson 74cl, Chris Steele-Perkins 29cl, Marilyn Silverstone 36br, S. Meiselas 34br **Missouri Historical Society, St Louis:** 39b **Museum of London/DK Picture Library:** 54tc, 54bl **Peter Newark's Pictures:** 39t **Olympic Co-ordination Authority:** Bob Peters, Highlight Studio 42c **Christine Osborne:** 37br **Oxford Scientific Films:** Ajay Desai 38t, David B. Fleetham 30br, Stan Osolinski 38c **PA News Photo Library:** 5br, 32br, 47b, David Cheskin 44acl **Peabody Museum, Harvard University:** Hillel Burger 39cl **Planet Earth Pictures:** 14 **Popperfoto:** 32bcl, 32tcr, 34tl, 40br, Dave Joiner 55bl, Gerard Fouet-AFP 34cl, Jeff J Mitchell 44al, Reuter 29cr, 34tr, 43bcr, 51br, 51tl **Rex Features:** 1, 3r, 4 al, tr, 5bl, 5ac, tl, 8bl, 8-9, 9br, 9cr, 9tr, 10br, c, bl, 11cl, 11cr, 11b, 12br, 12c 12bl, 12t, 13t, 13br, 13c, 13bl, 16c, 16bl, 16br, 17cr, 17tr, 17c, 18r, 18tl, 18bl, 19tr, 27c, 30bl, 59c, 60cr, 61tl, 61c, 65ca, 66t, 66bb, 67c, 67tr, 67tl, 68cl, 68cr, 69bl, 70tl, 70br, 71cr, 72tl, 72cl, 73tl,74r, 75br, 75tr, 77br, 77cl, 80bl, 81br, 82c, 83tl, 85cl, 87r, 87l, 88 bl, 90t, 91c, 94-95, Neal Lauron-Sipa Press 52bc, Peter Heinsath 49bl, Robert Trippett 52bc, Sipa Press 11 tl, 62b, 65br, 71cl, 76br, 77cr, 78 80tr, 80c, Sipa Press/Johan Kuus 43ar, Sipa

Sport 58, Sipa-Press/Zihnioglu 43al, Sipa/Sun Shine 51tr **Ann Ronan at Image Select:** 53t **Peter Sanders:** 35cr **Science & Society Picture Library:** 65bl **Science Photo Library:** 3l, 17bl, 73c, Geoff Tomlinson 17tl **The Slide File:** 41tl, 41tc, 41bl, 41cr **Spectrum Colour Library:** 32bc **Frank Spooner Pictures:** Rotolo-Liaison/Gamma 49 tl **Still Moving Picture Company:** Ken Paterson 44bc, S J Taylor 44bl **The Stock Market:** 30tc, 31br **Tony Stone Images:** 26-27, Cris Haigh 3c, 35bl, David Muench 50c, Dennis O'Clair 56cr, Ken Biggs 50bl, Kim Heacox 50cr, Mervyn Rees 42a **STSCi/AURA/NASA:** 14bl, E Karkoschka (University of Arizona) 15cr, J Hester, P Scowen (Arizona State University) 15t, J Morse (University of Colorado) 14r **Sygma:** Allan Tannenbaum 49 br, Archives Humanite Keystone 29 b, G Abegg 36 t, William Campbell 28 t **Syndics Today:** 51 **Telegraph Colour Library:** 35tl, David Kjaer 33c **Topham Picturepoint:** 4b, 8tl, 10t, 19 b, 2cr, 32bcr, 32tcl, 40bc, 41cl, 41 r, 43bl, 45cr, 46c, 47bl, 52cr, 60bl, 61bl, 67b, 69tl, 70bl, 71b, 72tr, 72br, 89c, 91t, Associated Press 9tl, 47br, Denis Brack 34bl, Martin McCullough 41br **Desmond Tutu:** 47t **UPI:** 43br **State Library of Victoria, Melbourne La Trobe Australian Manuscripts Collection:** 31cl **Vireo:** M.J. Rauzon 42br **Weald and Downland Open Air Museum:** Geoff Dann 46cr **White House Collection, copyright White House Historical Association:** 51, 56tr, 56tc

Special thanks to **The Flag Institute, Chester, UK,** for permission to reproduce flag images.